MEETING YOUR MATCH ONLINE:

The Complete Guide to Internet Dating and Dating Services — Including True Life Dating Stories

By Tamsen Butler

G YOUR MATCH ONLINE: THE COMPLETE
TO INTERNET DATING AND DATING SERVICES —
DING TRUE LIFE DATING STORIES

ght © 2009 Atlantic Publishing Group, Inc.
SW 6th Avenue • Ocala, Florida 34471 • Phone 800-814-1132 • Fax 352-622-1875
o site: www.atlantic-pub.com • E-mail: sales@atlantic-pub.com
AN Number: 268-1250

ISBN-13: 978-1-60138-152-1 ISBN-10: 1-60138-152-2

Library of Congress Cataloging-in-Publication Data

Butler, Tamsen, 1974-
  Meeting your match online : the complete guide to Internet dating and dating services, including true life date stories / Tamsen Butler.
    p. cm.
  Includes bibliographical references and index.
  ISBN-13: 978-1-60138-152-1 (alk. paper)
  ISBN-10: 1-60138-152-2 (alk. paper)
  1. Online dating. 2. Dating (Social customs). I. Title.

  HQ801.82.B88 2009
  646.7'702854678--dc22

                    2009027570

Printed in the United States

PROJECT MANAGER: Melissa Peterson • mpeterson@atlantic-pub.com
ASSISTANT EDITOR • Angela Pham • apham@atlantic-pub.com

Printed on Recycled Paper

We recently lost our beloved pet "Bear," who was not only our best and dearest friend but also the "Vice President of Sunshine" here at Atlantic Publishing. He did not receive a salary but worked tirelessly 24 hours a day to please his parents. Bear was a rescue dog that turned around and showered myself, my wife, Sherri, his grandparents Jean, Bob, and Nancy, and every person and animal he met (maybe not rabbits) with friendship and love. He made a lot of people smile every day.

We wanted you to know that a portion of the profits of this book will be donated to The Humane Society of the United States. *–Douglas & Sherri Brown*

The human-animal bond is as old as human history. We cherish our animal companions for their unconditional affection and acceptance. We feel a thrill when we glimpse wild creatures in their natural habitat or in our own backyard.

Unfortunately, the human-animal bond has at times been weakened. Humans have exploited some animal species to the point of extinction.

The Humane Society of the United States makes a difference in the lives of animals here at home and worldwide. The HSUS is dedicated to creating a world where our relationship with animals is guided by compassion. We seek a truly humane society in which animals are respected for their intrinsic value, and where the human-animal bond is strong.

Want to help animals? We have plenty of suggestions. Adopt a pet from a local shelter, join The Humane Society and be a part of our work to help companion animals and wildlife. You will be funding our educational, legislative, investigative and outreach projects in the U.S. and across the globe.

Or perhaps you'd like to make a memorial donation in honor of a pet, friend or relative? You can through our Kindred Spirits program. And if you'd like to contribute in a more structured way, our Planned Giving Office has suggestions about estate planning, annuities, and even gifts of stock that avoid capital gains taxes.

Maybe you have land that you would like to preserve as a lasting habitat for wildlife. Our Wildlife Land Trust can help you. Perhaps the land you want to share is a backyard— that's enough. Our Urban Wildlife Sanctuary Program will show you how to create a habitat for your wild neighbors.

So you see, it's easy to help animals. And The HSUS is here to help.

2100 L Street NW • Washington, DC 20037 • 202-452-1100
www.hsus.org

DEDICATION

To Monet and Abram,
my delightfully vibrant muses

TABLE OF CONTENTS

INTRODUCTION

What are you looking for in a potential mate? Do you have certain standards that must be met, and other things that are a little more flexible? Maybe your ideal mate is independent and spontaneous, or perhaps you envision falling deeply in love with someone who relies upon you to make decisions and dislikes making decisions without first mulling over every possible outcome.

You search for your potential sweetheart everywhere. Is the person standing in front of you at the grocery store your soul mate? Will your next blind date turn out to be "The One"? It is exciting to think that you may stumble upon the love of your life at any moment, but it is exhausting when, time and again, it becomes apparent that no one around you is completely compatible with what you are looking for. It would be so much easier if you could just input all your likes and dislikes into the computer and have your ideal mate appear before your eyes, right?

The good news is that *it is possible.*

Online dating is an amazing resource. Nowhere else can you sift through a massive catalog of single people and contact the ones you like while disregarding the ones you do not. You need not get dressed up to search online for a potential date, and you can do it when it suits your schedule. That means that if the only time you have available to look for love is in the early morning before heading to work, you will still have all the same options available to you if your schedule allows you to search on a Friday night. Online dating allows you to look for someone when it is convenient for you and in a way that also allows you be as selective as you like with who you contact and respond to.

In a hectic world, online dating is the perfect solution to finding the love of your life.

CASE STUDY: MELISSA'S STORY

"Not many people know that my husband and I met online using personal ads at Yahoo!™ Personals. We have this little joke that we actually met at Dairy Queen® since that's where we first met face-to-face.

I was not your typical 21-year-old! Sure, I met guys at bars and through work, but none of them were husband or father material, especially since I was a single mom. I began surfing through personal ads. In 2001, I don't remember having anything like Match.com® around or these other online dating sites, but even if they were, I would not have paid for the service back then, being that my money had to stretch pretty far. I met a few guys through personal ads they had posted — probably on Yahoo! Personals or something — but they were all let downs. Kenny had an ad posted — not that I remember the exact wording he used in his ad, but I am sure it had something to do with him being a 27-year-old divorced dad. I responded to his online ad, we exchanged pictures, and talked on the phone for about two weeks before we met. Because it was the middle of summer and he had his girls for visitation, we thought we would just do a big outing with all the kids and meet at Dairy Queen because if we happened to run out of things to talk about, we always had the kids as a distraction.

Ice cream was great and things seemed to be going well, so we each packed up in our cars and headed to the park to continue getting to know each other. Then, something happened: Kenny's youngest daughter had to use the restroom, and the park restrooms were closed off. I lived less than a mile away, and while I don't condone anyone going back to a date's house the first time you meet, this circumstance was special. Even though we really didn't know each other, I felt as though he was trustworthy. So we packed up and headed off to my place. The first date was pretty much done by then. The kids played for a short time and we said our goodbyes. I knew from that first date that this was the right man for me.

Kenny had been married twice already and had three daughters. I was a single, never-married mom of one little boy. Blended families are constantly given gloom and doom chances and believe me, the first few years were no picnic, but maybe it's true that third time's the charm! We were married in 2003. He adopted my son, I adopted his daughters, and so far, we have one baby together. There was never the question or opposition over parenting in our home, meaning his girls accepted me and my son accepted him from the start, and they all get along the same as if they had all been born of the same two people. They fight like cats and dogs, but they love each other completely, and Kenny and I will have many more stories to tell."

CHAPTER 1

Who and Why?

Who is online looking for love? The answer is simple: A wide variety of people. With online dating, you don't have to restrict your options to the singles living within your community or even within a 100-mile radius of your home. Online dating allows you to expand your options to scour the globe in your search for love. The decision is yours. Do you want to find someone nearby, or are you willing to look all over the world? Never before has it been so easy to meet single people within the specific geographic limitations of your choosing.

It doesn't stop with location. You can choose what kind of person you want to talk to depending on likes and dislikes, physical appearance, religious beliefs, and just about any other qualifying factors you may have. Are you looking for a tall, lanky person who is a Baptist and enjoys rollerblading?

This person could be online now. Do you want to meet someone who is petite yet muscular, wealthy, and a strict vegetarian? If you log on to a dating site and enter these specifications, chances are you'll have a few different people to choose from.

There is not one type of person who places personal ads online. The people who participate in online dating are as varied as the general population. The one single qualifying factor that unites the millions of people who date online is the fact that they all have access to a computer. If you want to find someone to date who has never touched a computer before, then online dating isn't for you. But if you're ready to meet people from a huge pool of different personalities, beliefs, and body types, all of whom also chose to use technology to help them find love, then online dating may be the perfect venue for you to find someone special.

Why do people turn to online dating when trying to meet someone? Although everyone has different reasons for logging on to find potential dates, there are plenty of good reasons why this is such a popular option.

People are busy. If you're working nine hours a day while also shouldering a long commute and everything else that comes with living as an adult, you probably don't have much time to devote to finding the love of your life. You can choose to simply wait for potential mates to stumble into your life but, if you are like most people, chances are you're a busy person and cannot spend a great deal of time devoted to meeting new people. As culture turns toward an electronic age — texting, e-mailing, and social networking online — you have probably found that more people are turning to quick and efficient ways to meet others. After all, it's much easier to sift through online dating profiles and shoot out a quick introductory e-mail than it is to wander through a bar and figure out how to get the attention of people who may or may not fit the mold of what you are looking for. Online dating simplifies the process for people who are too busy with life to meet people using traditional methods.

People are selective. You know what you are looking for, or at least you have a general idea of what is acceptable in a mate and what isn't. Online dating allows you to weed out the people who do not fit what you are looking for. Suppose you meet a person at a party and feel a connection to that person immediately. Will you feel comfortable enough to start listing your specific likes and dislikes right off the bat? Imagine what an aggressive conversation that would be: "I need someone who can support themselves financially and who goes to a church with similar beliefs as my church has. Do you enjoy baseball? You know, I could never date a person who doesn't like Mexican food." The other person would probably feel violated by your barrage of questions and demands. With online dating, you can state your likes and dislikes before you ever make contact with another person. You can be as selective as you want without offending a single person.

> "You wouldn't believe some of the e-mails I got...the atrocious writing. I finally posted a big warning of sorts that I was an ENGLISH teacher — hint, hint, check your spelling and grammar before hitting 'send.' Later, Jeff — who eventually became my husband — told me he re-read his e-mails two to three times, checking for errors before he sent them, worried that I'd reject him for a misspelled word or poorly punctuated sentence."
>
> -Lisa

People are curious. Poet Bryant H. McGill said, "Curiosity is one of the great secrets of happiness." Many people wonder if it is indeed possible to meet someone special online, and what type of people they could meet through a dating Web site. Commercials for popular dating sites make the claim that members are matched together using sophisticated technology, and for this reason, the perfect person is only a few mouse-clicks away. Some people begin their online search as a result of sheer curiosity. "Who can I meet online? Is it really possible to find someone special this way?" In some cases, these same people are pleased to find that they can indeed meet some great people online, some of whom become lifelong friends — and some of whom become lifelong partners. Some online dating sites offer free peeks at compatible singles, and for many people, this little peek is all they need to become intrigued enough to sign-up and start meeting new people.

But there are other reasons to turn to online dating. Newly divorced or widowed people may feel intimidated by the prospect of returning to the dating scene, especially if they were in their previous relationship for a long time. People who never thought they would need to get back into the swing of meeting new people and going on dates may have a desire to meet someone new — yet no idea how to go about it. For these people, online dating offers a safe way to reintegrate back into the singles scene without metaphorically going out on a limb. Searching through online profiles isn't nearly as intimidating as walking through a bar full of singles or asking friends to arrange a blind date.

With online dating, you can go at your own pace. You can decide to simply look through all the other profiles, or you can instead jump right in, post a profile, and let people contact you. This is a fantastic way to meet other people while also maintaining your acceptable level of comfort.

Are you ready to get started? Because many dating Web sites require membership fees, you'll want to review which is best for you before signing-up. You may be anxious to jump right in and sign-up for several Web sites at once, but keep in mind that it may be best to start with one or two sites and then decide if you want to add more into the mix. You may soon find that while you like the format of one site, you prefer the type of singles on another. It won't take you long to settle into one particular Web site that suits your needs and is easy-to-use.

Take a look at the review in Chapter 2 of some of the most

popular online dating sites available before signing up for one.

Online dating proves to be even more popular during slow economic times. Many dating sites have reported increased membership numbers since the economic downturn in fall 2008. It seems that people are looking to improve their personal life in order to compensate for their economic woes; it is estimated that more than 60 million people visit online dating sites each month.

In December 2008, Reuters® spoke with Gian Gonzaga, senior research scientist at eHarmony. "On days when the U.S. Dow Jones industrial (average) went down by a lot, by more than 100 points, more people were likely to log in and spend more time on the site," he reported. "It makes a lot of sense. People seek out companionship in times of stress. Studies repeatedly show that being in a relationship can help a person's psychological and physical health."

www.Match.com agrees with this assessment. In November 2008, the site reported their largest membership growth in seven years. **www.Perfectmatch. com** also has seen a 47 percent increase in membership numbers. In a Reuters interview, Thomas Enraght-Mooney, CEO of Match.com, said, "During these trying times, people are looking for hope in their inbox."

In a poll conducted on behalf of **www.eHarmony.com**, 57 percent of people polled said that the downturn made them worried about their love lives, with younger respondents most worried about how their economic situation would impact their love lives. However, these respondents were also more likely to seek out relationships if they were currently single. Older respondents, who were more likely to already be married, were more worried that financial problems would negatively impact their marriages.

Many people also find that online dating also is a great way to save money during a time when funds are sparse. More people are resorting to chatting online or over the phone than through traditional dating. With movie ticket prices and other traditional dating options at an all-time high, the dating scene has become more expensive than ever. With monthly membership fees averaging $40 per month, online dating is a much more viable option for people seeking a relationship.

Location, Location, Location

Suppose you live in a small town or a rural location where there simply aren't very many single people. This is a common scenario in smaller towns: Everyone seems to already knows each other, and if you don't find any of few available singles appealing, you're out of luck. On the other hand, maybe you live in a large metropolitan area where the majority of people rush around and don't take the time to meet other people because they are either too busy or are secure with their existing social circle. In either scenario, it can be difficult to meet prospective dates.

Online dating solves this problem. Location is an issue only if you want it to be when it comes to looking for someone online. With the Internet as your tool, you can search for a compatible match across the globe in a country you have never visited or perhaps that you didn't even know existed.

On the other hand, don't make the mistake of believing that online dating is only suitable for people who have geographic restrictions. You may live in an area that has a bustling, thriving single's scene, but that doesn't mean you can't benefit from meeting people online.

CASE STUDY: MIKE'S STORY

"I enjoyed Internet dating for years because I was able to maintain the proper perspective — embracing the adventure, while managing the expectations. I met my first wife, a Chinese engineer here in California, on the old Love@AOL® service. When she abruptly ended our five-year marriage just days after becoming a U.S. citizen (yes, that really does happen), I had no hesitation about returning to the online single's world. Through **www.Match.com** and Yahoo! Personals (**http://personals.yahoo.com**), I quickly met some very nice people and had some great dates.

After my previous experience, however, I certainly wasn't looking for another foreign connection. So when I was pinged by a Chinese doctor named Sarah on Yahoo! in mid-2006, my first thought was, 'Right; just what I need — a recent immigrant 2,000 miles away in Wisconsin, of all places.' But then I saw her photos. I'm a pushover for a great smile, and hers could melt glaciers. And her imperfect note was somehow eloquent. Sarah had never considered an American guy, but she liked what I'd written in my profile about how much I had loved traveling in China during my marriage and the appreciation I had developed for Chinese history and culture. And, as she confessed much later, my smile had melted her, too.

So we connected. After a few weeks of e-mails, we began talking on the phone every night. We were cautious because we were both going through divorces, but those laughter-filled calls began stretching longer and longer. Finally, in late summer, just as all the legalities were completed, she courageously flew out to California — ostensibly to visit a family friend, but really to meet me. We walked in the redwoods, we ate ice cream, and on our third date, we kissed ... and it was magic. After kissing the wrong girls for decades, I finally found out what it was like to kiss that one right lady and feel the world turn upside-down. It turned out to be the greatest moment (okay, more like 20 minutes) of my life. We married less than six months later.

We laugh today about the extraordinary odds against ever meeting each other, how so many pieces of luck had to fall into place just right, and how this little miracle could only have happened online. We plan to keep on laughing — and savoring all that luck — for the next 50 years or so."

Real or Fake?

With so many people online, it's safe to assume that not everyone tells the absolute truth on their profiles. While some people tell little lies in an attempt to catch the eye of a potential mate — such as fibbing about age or maybe not telling the entire truth when it comes to weight — there are some people online who completely fabricate profiles that are far cries from reality. For these people, online dating is amusement and isn't a real attempt to meet someone at all. Instead, perusing ads online and communicating with people is more of an entertaining sport than anything else.

Take solace in the fact that these people are a tiny minority of the online dating population. The potential of bumping into one of these people online should not stop you from starting your online dating adventure. After all, when you walk into a singles bar, there is a chance that you will meet someone who tells you a stream of lies, but this doesn't deter you from continuing your search.

The majority of people with profiles online post them online because they have a genuine desire to meet someone new. Trust your intuition. If a profile seems fishy or fake, simply move on to the next one. Don't let the fear of a fake profile stop you from potentially meeting the person of your dreams.

Nothing to Lose

Online dating offers an initial anonymity that you simply can't find in the traditional dating scene. The ability to peruse databases of singles is like being able to walk through a singles bar without making yourself vulnerable. On the other side of the coin is the fact that there are no hurt feelings on the part of the people with profiles you glaze over because, in most cases, they don't even know that someone has looked and disregarded their profile.

Online dating can be a safe way to see what kinds of people are available. If you are re-entering the dating scene after a long absence, such as after a divorce or after spending time focused on your career or education, perusing a database of singles can be a reassuring act. You will likely encounter a wide variety of people, including attractive, accomplished people who will catch your eye and prove to you that there are still fish in the sea. If the database you look through does not contain anyone who appeals to you, there are plenty of other sites online that have databases full of people who may be better-suited for you.

Dealing with Backlash

Online dating is now a mainstream practice and is becoming increasingly common as a way to meet a mate. On the other hand, there are some stigmas attached to online dating — especially among people who have not dated in today's society, such as grandparents and parents — that some people may be eager to point out to you once they find out you have a dating profile online.

If you decide to tell people that you are trying online dating, be prepared to get an earful of opinions. It is usually those who have never actually tried online dating who seem to have the most adamant opinions about it. You may be told by friends and family that online dating is for desperate people, or that it is dangerous. But the fact is that people fear the things they don't understand, so take negative comments with a grain of salt.

If you have a concerned friend or family member who urges you to avoid online dating out of concern for your safety or reputation, you may want to allow that person to sit with you and look over your shoulder as you peruse an online dating single's database. When that person sees how normal the vast majority of people appear to be, it may alleviate any concerns. On the other hand, some people simply hold steadfast onto their opinions and beliefs — even if the beliefs are unfounded and unmerited — so there may be nothing you can do to sway their negative outlook.

Keep in mind that as long as you are a single adult, you don't need to justify your foray into online dating to anyone. Your parents, friends, and the people you work with may have opinions. If you're older, your children may loudly express their concerns that you may get taken advantage of by someone you meet online. Try to take everyone's concern as a compliment that they care about you, but don't feel as though you need to live your life to please anyone but yourself. Ultimately, the decision of whether to participate in online dating is up to you. You'll soon learn that there are a lot of great people online who are genuinely looking for a solid relationship with someone who is compatible with them, and that the abnormal and unstable people are the minority.

Assure the people who are concerned for you that you plan on using utmost caution when dealing with people you meet online. Answer their questions and be open about the process. Consistently portray a positive outlook about the online dating experience, and you may just sway a single friend or family member to join you online.

Still, if you know for sure that the people around you are going to be critical and unsupportive about your online dating, it may be best to simply keep it to yourself. You and your future mate can reveal to everyone how you really met when you're celebrating your wedding.

CHAPTER 2

Which Site is Right for You?

While you certainly don't need to limit yourself to one dating Web site, it is a good idea to set a limit of just a couple. Why is this important? First of all, there are usually fees associated with joining a Web site and gaining full access, so unless money is no object, you will want to limit the number of sites you join for financial reasons alone. Furthermore, you don't want to spread yourself too thin. You may soon find that looking through databases of singles can become time-consuming. After all, you may stumble upon someone compatible with you at any time while searching through available singles, so it can become quite addicting. Additionally, it can be easier to concentrate on finding a compatible match when you limit your searches to one or two Web sites.

Before you decide on any particular Web sites, it's worth it to take a look at a few different sites. Different sites offer different features, so if you find that you don't like the format of one site or the selection of singles on another, rest assured that there are plenty of other Web sites offering the features you are looking for. Don't be afraid to shop through a variety of Web sites, but, ultimately, you should settle down with one or two sites that have all the features and types of people you are looking for.

There are some dating sites that are very specific to a particular subculture. If you have especially particular likes and dislikes and need someone who can fit well with what you're looking for, you may want to take a look at dating sites that tailor searches to your wants and needs. For example, active duty military personnel often live a demanding life and need someone who can understand this. For these people, a Web site such as **www.Military Singles.com**® can be a great choice because it is specifically designed for military singles and those interested in meeting them. This is not to say that there are no suitable singles for military personnel on other dating Web sites, but sites that are created with a specific focus can eliminate a lot of searching.

The same principle can be applied to a variety of other people with particular preferences. If you are looking to meet someone of the same sex, some sites are designed for that. Though some of the larger dating Web sites offer same-sex matches, you may find a much larger selection to choose from by visiting a site like **www.Gay.com**®. Likewise, if you want to date someone who is passionate about the same hobby as you, then you can stress this preference within your profile on a general dating Web site, or you can try to find a dating site filled with those who have the same passions as you do.

You may be surprised to find there are numerous dating sites dedicated to certain lifestyles and activities. Single parents can meet other single parents at **www.SingleParent-Meet.com**®. People who have been affected by cancer can meet other people in similar circumstances at **www.CisforCupid.com**. Singles who have mental disorders can meet similar singles at **www.NoLongerLonely.com**. There is even a dating Web site specific to artists: **www.Single ArtistDating.com**.

Another great example of Web sites catering to a certain population are those dedicated to certain religious beliefs. On sites like **www.ChristianSingles.com**, you won't find as many blatantly raunchy profiles as you might on a mainstream dating site. Although there are many different denominations and levels of faith, people using a Web site like this one are typically looking for like-minded singles who share similar values and a desire to date a Christian. You can specify your religious preferences on almost all of the dating Web sites, but by subscribing to a site specifically designed for faith-based dating — such as **www.LutheranFriendFinder.com**® (for Lutherans), **www. SalaamLove.com** (for Muslims), and **www.OldeSouls.com** (for Pagans) — you may be able to pinpoint a potential mate faster because you can assume that everyone registered on the site has similar beliefs to you. In fact, many of the faith-based dating Web sites have a strict code of ethics that all members are expected to adhere to. While this certainly isn't foolproof, it may be enough to discourage someone with polar-opposite beliefs from registering on the site.

Do you need to use a Web site that is designed specifically for certain people and certain tastes? Plenty of people have found love on sites that offer a diverse variety of singles, just as there are success stories for sites that cater to specific groups of people. Much of it boils down to which you personally prefer. You want to find a site that offers a format you like and has a large number of singles who are compatible with you.

It's likely you will soon find that the vast majority of dating Web sites are quite formulaic: You specify who you are and what you are looking for, then you peruse eligible singles. You contact the ones you find appealing and reply to those who contact you. On the other hand, you may also discover quickly that some Web sites are simply better than others. You will develop preferences regarding how you like to conduct a search for singles within a database, as well as how you like information from a profile to be presented.

However, keep in mind that there isn't one specific dating Web site that reigns supreme above all others because there are so many different people with varying tastes. Ask two different people active in the online dating community what their favorite Web site is, and you will probably receive two different responses — for many different reasons. Essentially, it boils down to this: The best dating Web site is the one that you prefer above all others. It should have a format that you find appealing and a database full of singles that have the potential to be compatible with you.

Be Selective

You don't want to blanket the Internet with your dating profile. If a potential mate finds you on multiple sites, he or she is likely to assume one of two things: You are either very thorough — or very desperate. Instead of signing up for every dating site you can find (which would certainly use up a great deal of your time and money), you should stick to one or two sites that you like.

How do you decide which Web sites to use? Ask yourself these questions:

Do I *like* the site? You'll quickly get a feeling for the various Web sites you visit. Whether it's the format of the site or the sequence of events that take place when you visit the site, it probably won't take you long to decide if you like a site or not. You may not be able to pinpoint exactly what your reasoning is, but pay attention to which sites seem easiest to use.

Is the selection of singles appealing and abundant? If a site has ease of use, but you don't seem to be able to find any suitable singles on the site, then it probably isn't the site for you.

Remember that the whole point of your quest is to find someone special. It doesn't matter if you adore the format of a certain Web site; if there aren't any appealing singles on the site, then the site isn't helping you reach your intended goal.

What is the cost of the site? Although cost isn't a major consideration for everyone, most people do not want to spend a small fortune when joining a dating site. On the other hand, you certainly don't want to join a particular Web site only because it's the cheapest of the bunch. You must weigh all the considerations and find a happy balance. The site you eventually settle on may cost a little more than some of the other sites you visit, but if the format of the Web site is appealing and there is a wide variety of suitable singles, then the extra cost may be worth it. You should also consider other monetary aspects with the site. Is membership automatically renewed upon expiration? Are there extra features that aren't accessible to you unless you pay even more? Meeting your match online should not drain your savings account, but you should be prepared to spend some money for access to the best sites.

Does the site cater to my lifestyle and what I'm looking for? Some dating sites are very specific with regards to the population the site caters to, while other dating sites welcome all singles. Check out Web sites that offer singles who have the same interests as you, but be sure to also try some of the more generalized Web sites to see who is in the database. Searching for dates online is a great time to allow yourself to broaden your horizons a little. Maybe you have always dated a certain type of person without much success. This may be the best time to meet some people who deviate a little from what you're used to. After all, remember that Albert Einstein defined insanity as "doing the same thing over and over again and expecting different results." If that's what you have been doing with regards to selecting people to date, maybe it's time to try something new.

Take your time perusing the various Web sites. After you settle on one or two Web sites to frequent, keep in mind that there are plenty of other sites out there. For this reason, if you find yourself getting disenchanted with one site, you may want to cancel your membership and move on to a different dating Web site. That is one of the great things about online dating: The possibilities seem nearly endless.

Getting Started with Any Site

When you decide upon a particular dating site, you need to read the user's agreement before signing up. You want to make sure that you fully understand what you are about to get yourself into before supplying your e-mail address and credit card number. Why is this important? When you join the membership of a dating site, you agree to abide by the user's agreement. This is a legally binding agreement. There are certain things you agree to do — like pay your monthly dues — and certain things you agree to not do — like place naked photos of yourself on your profile

— and by agreeing to the user's agreement, you are required to follow the rules set forth by the Web site. Most Web sites will not allow you to join without first clicking that you have read and agreed to the terms of the Web site. Don't glaze over this agreement. It may seem like a bunch of legal drivel, but if you don't take the time to read it through, you might find yourself with automatic payments far beyond what you thought you were originally signing up for, or you might discover that programs have been downloaded to your computer that you didn't realize you authorized. By confirming that you have read and agreed to the user's agreement, you're legally allowing the Web site to do whatever it states.

If you read a user's agreement and don't understand something contained within the wording, contact the customer service department of the Web site and ask for clarification. Don't simply agree to the terms and then ask questions later. By then, it's too late to rescind your agreement. Online dating can be a lot of fun and a great way to meet new people, but you always have to keep in mind that you enter into a contractual relationship with the dating sites you join. Know the terms of the user's agreement before you click the box to signify your acceptance of the terms.

If the site allows you to look through the database of singles before signing up for a membership, be sure to take advantage of this feature. It can be disappointing to take the time to fill out a profile and pay membership dues only to find that there really aren't any compatible singles featured on the Web site or, worse yet, that the few appealing singles on the site haven't logged on to their accounts for several months, signifying that they have either moved on to another site or stopped looking for whatever reason.

For any dating Web site, check out whatever features you are allowed to access before actually joining the site. For some sites there will be a wide variety of features, but others are very restrictive about what they will allow non-users to access. Be wary of any dating Web site that does not offer at least a small peek at the features on the Web site before demanding payment, and if any Web site doesn't seem "quite right," don't sign up at all.

CASE STUDY: MONIQUE'S STORY

"Brian and I met on **www.Match.com** back in November 2005, two days after Thanksgiving. After years of dating in my 20s, I just hadn't managed to meet the right guy. My friend Anna kept encouraging me to try online dating, but I always thought it was a weird and sort of "creepy" way to meet someone. I guess I was sort of a traditionalist and figured I would just meet someone through friends or at a bar, and that would be it. But finally, I decided to give Match.com a try.

After having my profile up for less than a week, I met Brian. We e-mailed only a few times before meeting, and we didn't even talk on the phone until a few hours before our first date. But once we met, I knew that he was really different from the other men that I had dated and that we were really on the same page about so many things. Our relationship turned serious right away, and we were engaged seven months later. Our wedding was held where I grew up in Buffalo, New York, on May 5, 2007. Brian's wedding band is inscribed with 'my perfect match' to signify the way we met."

Familiarizing Yourself

Some dating Web sites offer tutorials to help new users get started, but most of the sites are easily navigated and can be figured out without much hassle. For the majority of dating Web sites, your first big step will be to create your profile, but there are other features on these sites that you may want to have a look at before actually posting your complete profile. Take a look to see if the site offers extra features such as forums, blogs, online chat capabilities, and Webcams. Some of the larger dating sites offer a library of information for singles to read. Topics you may find within these resource libraries include suggestions for crafting an appealing profile, how to make a good first impression on a date, and tips for increasing your chances of having a long-term relationship. Some of the larger dating sites will offer expert advice within these resource libraries, while other dating Web sites may offer general tips that are not from an expert source.

Whether you utilize the extra features or not, it is worth it to check them out. Maybe you have never used a Webcam before and you feel intimidated by the thought of sitting in front of your computer's camera talking to someone you have never met in person. Upon actually trying it, however, you may discover that you actually prefer it to all other available lines of communication on the dating site because it makes the person you are connecting with seem more authentic and accessible. On the other hand, if you discover that you just don't like using the Webcam, then at least you know that you gave it a shot and know with a complete degree of certainty that you don't like it. You won't have to worry that you are missing something.

Undoubtedly, you want to jump right into searching through the singles that are online, but before you do this, you need to arm yourself with the right tools. You should realize that almost everyone who you initiate contact with will want to check out your profile before replying to your note. Avoid sending out a blanket of e-mails and other contact requests to singles until you have a complete profile in place. Why is this so important? There are a few different reasons.

First and foremost, most of the people involved in online dating have to be a little wary of initiated contact that comes from someone who does not have a completed profile. No matter how compelling your initial e-mail is, if the person you contact can't go to your profile and learn more about you, then there is a good chance you will never receive a response. This is especially true if the person you contact has been burned by someone in the past who was initially vague.

Second, some singles online spend a great deal of time crafting the perfect profile, so when someone doesn't bother to put any effort into a profile, it can be off-putting. Think about it this way: You are a great catch and are worthy of attention. Shouldn't your profile be indicative of this? Aren't you worthy of an intriguing profile?

The last thing you want to do is to convey the idea that you don't think you deserve to spend time perfecting your profile. When you initiate contact with other singles, the very first thing most of them do is have a look at your profile. What do you want them to see? What message are you trying to send to potential dates?

The capabilities of your computer can either enhance or limit your experience with online dating. An old computer that runs slowly — or an Internet connection that is sluggish — can make the process painfully time-consuming.

Yes, you want to jump right in and start talking to single people who peak your interest. You don't have to go at a snail's crawl in order to do it, but you should use a little caution and take your time preparing your profile so that you will present yourself in the best light to the people who will see your profile online.

Most people who have spent some time with online dating find that the way they interact with other singles online changes and evolves over time. They look back on how they first went about contacting other singles and they realize that they should have done things a little differently. Always remember that you're not running a race. Even if you want to be with someone as soon as possible, there is really no rush when it comes to online dating. Why not enjoy the process? When else do you have the capability to search through thousands of profiles of people who are willing to allow complete strangers a small glimpse into their lives? Indeed, if you haven't yet figured it out, then it's time to make this realization: Online dating can be *fun*.

CASE STUDY: SUSAN'S STORY

"It all began on December 15, 2005. I decided to get a subscription to a rock group in Yahoo! Groups (**http://groups.yahoo.com**). I was lonely and thought maybe e-mailing with a group of people with interests common to mine would be good. So I sent my first e-mail introducing myself: My name, what I do for a living, my age, my music interests, blah, blah. Most of the other members gave me a nice, warm welcome, and I was happy. Suddenly someone sent an e-mail saying: 'I don't know why people who have received invitations nobody sent keep joining this group!' I was outraged! How dare he? Didn't I have a right to be there? It was a public group, after all! So I checked with the moderator and he said I shouldn't worry about it.

But I'm not one to take these kinds of things quietly, so I replied to his e-mail saying I had every right to be there. He wrote back, and it was a week of aggressive e-mails back and forth. At some point I decided to start ignoring his e-mails and focused on participating in the rest of the group's e-mailings. A couple of weeks went by and I received a private e-mail from him asking if I could translate some articles for him and how much I'd charge him. I replied as coldly as I possibly could.

He started sending e-mails, at first on this matter and then changing subjects to more personal matters. He told me he was eight years older than me and separated with four kids and a grandson. He asked about my own story and, in the end, I started telling him some things. We exchanged instant message contact info and began chatting at every hour. When we exchanged pictures, he kept saying I was gorgeous — which definitely helped my ego — so I started feeling good things about this guy.

One day, he asked for my telephone number and we spoke on the phone for quite a long time. On January 20, there was a group meeting, and there I saw him for the first time. We barely talked that night because we sat on opposite ends of the table, and each of us was talking to a different group of people. At one point he texted me and offered to buy me a soda. Of course, I said yes, and a few minutes later, a waitress brought it to me. That was strange.

On February 15, he had a show, as he was a rock singer, so I went. In the meantime, we had been having long talks on the phone and through IM, so we had begun to know each other pretty well. At the show he was surrounded by his friends, so I barely got to see him. Later, we all went for drinks and this girl was throwing herself at him the whole time, but he only had eyes for me. He started pretending to be drunk to get away from her.

CASE STUDY: SUSAN'S STORY

That night ended with no big news, but on the way home he texted me for the one-hour-long bus ride. A few days later, I had a big problem at home and he called me right then — we spent four hours talking. That month's phone bill was enormous! When finishing the call, we arranged to meet the following day because I was quite affected by what had happened at home.

On February 28, we met at a public place and sat and talked for hours on end. Finally, he just looked at me pretty seriously and kissed me in the sweetest, most romantic way. After that, we started seeing each other every other day. By April 7, he was moving in with my son, my mom, and me, even though we knew that it wasn't going to be easy. Every other weekend, his three youngest came over, which was certainly messy.

We lasted for almost three years together, but in the end, lots of personal stuff got in the way and it didn't work out. While it lasted, it was good and worth every effort."

Internet Technology

If you aren't well-versed in using a computer, don't worry; the dating sites make everything as user-friendly as possible. If you can navigate e-mail, then chances are you will have no problem figuring out how to navigate most dating sites. People who are not necessarily computer-savvy should keep a few things in mind before venturing onto dating sites in order to get the best experience possible.

System Requirements

If you have an old computer, or one that does not run very well, you may find that online dating can become frustrating.

If you are spending several minutes waiting for a Web page to load, you may quickly grow bored or frustrated with the process. Pages that won't load, pop-ups that interrupt your online dating session, and your computer locking up or freezing altogether can certainly ruin the online dating experience.

Some sites may not load properly if your computer can't handle all the data presented by the site. The more images on the site, the more slowly your computer may load the page. With a newer computer in good working order with a quick, reliable Internet connection, this is not much of an issue, but if your computer has been around for a while and your Internet connection is inconsistent, then this can be a definite problem.

Internet Connection

A dial-up Internet connection can take a lot longer than a high speed Internet connection. How do you know if your Internet connection is dial-up? If your computer has an attachment that goes through your phone line and presents different phone numbers for you to try to connect through, then you have a dial-up connection. Some older computers will still make audible noises when connecting to the Internet through a dial-up connection, and this sounds like a squeak or squeals. You know you have a dial-up connection if a phone call coming in interrupts your Internet session by knocking off the connection.

If you plan on spending a great deal of time perusing online dating sites, you may want to upgrade your Internet to a high-speed connection. The difference that it makes in getting connected to Web sites, as well as how quickly the pages load, may amaze you.

Your Computer

If you spend any time online for whatever reason, you need to have anti-virus software on your computer. Some software can be downloaded for free (such as AVG, available at **http://free.avg.com**), but it is usually worth it to purchase a program that includes online updates and assistance, like McAfee® or Norton Antivirus™.

What is a computer virus? It's a program that is installed into your computer without your knowledge. It can be a mere annoyance that nabs the e-mail addresses out of your e-mail system and sends out advertisements to your contacts, or it can be a malicious program that destroys your entire system. Unfortunately, it is all too easy to wind up with a computer virus simply by surfing the Internet. All it takes is clicking on a certain link or downloading what you think is a picture for one of these programs to wind up on your computer. In fact, if a friend or business contact has a virus on his or her computer, an e-mail from this person may infect your computer and then spread on to your contacts as well. This is why you absolutely need to have an anti-virus program installed on your computer *before* you start venturing into online dating.

Be wary of attachments sent to you from other online daters.

Suppose you request a photo from someone you are speaking to online, so the person sends you a photo as an attachment. You download the attachment to view the photo, but it turns out the file was infected with a virus, and now your computer is infected. The sender may not have even intended to send a virus to you — or perhaps that was the plan all along — but an anti-virus program that screens incoming e-mails and attachments can stop this sort of thing from infiltrating your system. Request that the person simply posts the new picture to his or her profile or uses an online photo database to allow you access to see the picture without the risk of a virus.

A Snail's Pace

If your computer runs incredibly slow, and it isn't the Internet connection or a computer virus causing the problem, it may be that your computer is older or does not have sufficient memory. You can try running a system scan or defragmentation to try to speed the computer up a little, and sometimes, deleting unneeded files and programs can speed up your computer quite a bit. Video games in particular can take up a lot of memory, so if you have many games on your computer, you may want to delete the ones that you don't play in order to make some room for other things.

If all else fails, it may just be time to get a new computer. If your computer is more than a few years old, then you may be surprised to discover how much faster a new computer can operate, as well as how inexpensive a new computer can be when you find a great sale or discount. If you don't know much about buying computers, be sure to tell the salesperson that your main purpose is to access the Internet because some computers are better than others for access. The salesperson can steer you toward a suitable computer that will have you hopping from one profile to another with the greatest of ease.

CASE STUDY: LUKE AND MICHELLE'S STORY

Luke Ward, age 32, from Buffalo, New York, and Michelle Solomon, age 30, from Long Island, New York, met through **www. Friendster.com**. While Friendster is more of a social networking site than a dating site, if you noted that you were single, a "Single in Your Area" sidebar would appear whenever you were signed on. This sidebar featured a rotating cast of the opposite sex (if that's what you stated you preferred) that were single, lived near you, and were separated from you by less than three degrees of separation. It turned out that Michelle and Luke had friends that knew each other, so they kept popping up on each other's "Single in Your Area" sidebar. Michelle "bookmarked" Luke and made it visible to him, so she wasn't too surprised to get his e-mail two weeks later. He claims, however, that he never saw the bookmark and was drawn in by her "classy" main photo that showed her pretending to drink two Coronas at once.

It turned out that Luke and Michelle lived a whole two and a half blocks away from each other, and they met for the first time on February 2, 2006, to get a drink. That date lasted four hours and, when Luke dropped Michelle off at her door, he proclaimed, "I had fun?" This seemed to confuse him. This was an indication of the types of dates that they both had been on prior to meeting. Thankfully, Luke was not confused when he asked Michelle to move in with him in November 2006, nor when he proposed in January 2008. Luke and Michelle were married on September 14, 2008, and look forward to spending the rest of their lives together.

CHAPTER 3

What Sites Are Out There?

While it's not feasible to review every single dating site available online — there are new sites popping up constantly — you may have an easier time choosing which sites to explore by taking a look at the basic offerings of some of the more popular dating sites on the Web. Rest assured that if you don't like the look of any of these sites, there are plenty of other sites catering to a wide variety of people. Keep in mind that the most popular dating sites will have a larger number of singles to choose from, but sites specific to certain hobbies, religious beliefs, or other defining characteristics may have members who have specific traits you are looking for.

Site Reviews

www.Perfectmatch.com®

Perfectmatch will e-mail initial matches to you, but only after you have submitted your information, including likes and dislikes. You will answer questions about who you are and what you are looking for in a potential partner. Get ready to answer questions regarding your environmental stance, your religious beliefs, and your hobbies. The Duet® analysis — which is the compatibility analysis tool featured on this site designed to match you with someone who is suitable for you — will also ask questions about how you would react to situations like falling in love and your level of comfort with discussing problems with a partner.

After you finish the questionnaire, you'll be prompted to purchase a membership before viewing any matches on the site. You can purchase the membership in different monthly increments. Depending on which membership you buy, this site offers a Perfectmatch Guarantee that guarantees you will receive a certain number of compatible matches within a certain amount of time, otherwise you will receive a partial refund based on how many matches you receive and how long of a membership you initially purchased. Once in a while, this Web site offers special discounted deals, but the Perfectmatch Guarantee may not apply to these specially-priced memberships.

Warning! Perfectmatch will automatically renew your membership fees upon the expiration date of your current membership unless you contact them and stop the automatic renewal.

You will not be able to fully peruse the database of singles on Perfectmatch if you don't sign-up and pay the fees associated with membership. You can see the initial matches based on your questionnaire, but you will not be able to contact these members until after you pay the fee.

Perfectmatch doesn't guarantee a huge variety of singles, but it does make the claim that you will be carefully matched with other singles that are compatible with you. The compatibility tools used on the Web site are based on academic and scientific research over the last 30 years, so people who want to take a scientific approach to finding a compatible single may like the approach used by this site.

What's good about Perfectmatch: The detailed survey allows you to get matched with someone based on several aspects of personality.

What you may not like about Perfectmatch: The questions on the initial survey are presented without options to clarify your answers, which may leave you feeling a little boxed-in.

An organizational psychologist I knew used eHarmony because he believed so strongly in personality testing. We were just all shocked that somebody like him would use an online dating service, but he completely bought into it and liked it. Even if you're not using a dating Web site that focuses on the personality assessment, knowing your actual personality tendencies, and doing something objective that actually tells you about yourself, should be really useful.

-Dr. Todd Darnold

www.eHarmony.com®

eHarmony requires a thorough questionnaire before allowing you access to the database of singles. The questionnaire includes questions regarding your religious beliefs, your temperament, and your physical appearance. Although the questionnaire includes a large number of questions and may seem a little daunting, completing the questionnaire actually doesn't take a very long time as long as you respond with your very first reaction to the questions. Mulling over the questions before responding will lengthen the process considerably and may result in you answering the questions as you want people to see you as opposed to your true self. If you have ever taken a personality test before, you will recognize the format. The test is designed to find out who you fundamentally are as a person so you can be matched with singles that are compatible with you in a deep, meaningful way. It isn't all about being attracted to someone else or having similar lifestyles; on eHarmony, the goal is to find out who you *really* are so you can be matched with someone who will love the real you.

While filling out the questionnaire, it may seem as though you are answering the same questions over and over again. Just try to keep answering the questions as honestly as possible because this is how you will eventually get matched with other singles. If you are serious about your online dating experience with eHarmony, then you should consider the questionnaire to be a very important step in the process.

You will also notice that some of the questions on the question-naire seem a little odd, such as whether you ever feel as though you are being plotted against by people. These questions aren't meant to be amusing. They are valid questions that may make most people pause, but should be asked in case someone feels compelled to answer them with a confident "Yes, people are in-deed plotting against me!" As you work your way through the questionnaire, keep an eye on the bar to the right of the ques-tions. This will show you how much progress you've made. It's best to work through the questions without spending too much time wondering why you're being asked certain things. If the questionnaire becomes too lengthy for your liking, you can save your responses and log back on at another time to finish.

When you are completing the questionnaire, it's important to keep in mind that there is an actual system in place that is de-signed to match with someone who is compatible with you, not with the person *you want to be*. For this reason, you have to make sure that you answer the questions as truthfully as possi-ble. For example, if you are asked about how often you feel sad, don't glaze over the fact that maybe you feel sad quite a bit. The questions aren't designed to make you feel bad about yourself; they are designed to help you find someone that is compatible with you. Don't lie! The matching system offered by eHarmony will prove ineffective if you don't answer all the questions as truthfully and authentically as possible. You may get matched with someone else based on the untruthful answers you give, and this is a recipe for a failed relationship right off the bat.

When you have completed the questionnaire you will receive a brief listing of matches. You won't be able to see their photos. The initial contact with these matches is set by eHarmony; you can ask your match five pre-written questions and await a response. You won't be able to send the questions — or initiate any form of communication with any of your matches — until you subscribe to the site. When you are ready to initiate contact, you will follow a series of steps before the two of you actually talk on the phone. These steps are based on the compatibility system set up by eHarmony and can go relatively quickly if you and the other person work your way through the steps quickly. On the other hand, people who check their accounts infrequently may find that it takes much longer to get to the point to where you can directly contact the other eHarmony member.

You can choose from a few different membership options, including a year-long membership or a membership that only lasts one month.

What's good about eHarmony: Like Perfectmatch, the detailed survey allows you to be matched with someone based on several aspects of personality. The step-by-step process that must be followed in order to achieve phone contact can also help weed out singles who aren't compatible.

What you may not like about eHarmony: You cannot sift through the database at your leisure because this site specifies who you have access to. Additionally, you may wind up rejected by eHarmony as a member for a variety of reasons that aren't specified by the Web site.

www.True.com®

As you fill out the questionnaire for True, a counter appears in the upper, right-hand corner that tells you how many potential matches you have. As you further clarify your wants and needs, the counter starts to drop. For this reason, you may start out excited because you have thousands of potential matches in the beginning, but as you complete the survey, the number drops.

Upon completion of the survey, you'll be asked to sign-up for a free trial, but will also be asked to provide a credit card number so your membership can be expanded when the free trial expires. You can still view your initial matches and have a look at their profiles and photos without signing-up for the free trial, but you will not be able to contact any of your matches until you have signed-up.

True also offers a chat room feature that will pop-up once you have completed the questionnaire. This allows you to chat live with compatible singles who are online. Keep in mind that the prompt to join the chat room does not mean that any of the people chatting on the site have been prescreened as compatible to you, but instead that there simply may be someone of the opposite sex who is also online and looking to chat.

Though chatting online can be a lot of fun and a great way to meet some new people, if you are new to chatting, you should be aware that some people use this feature as a way to initiate sexual conversations with other people. If you find yourself chatting with someone and notice that the conversation is starting to get a little too spicy for you, either click off or inform the other chatter that this is not what you're looking for. On the other hand, if this is exactly what you're looking for, then the chat feature at True can be a lot of fun for you.

You might find a wide variety of singles on this network, including people who are only looking for dates and not necessarily for a long-term commitment. Be sure to look closely at the profiles to find out what they are looking for before initiating contact because you don't want to contact someone who only wants a one-time date if you are looking to fall in love.

What's good about True: The chat feature makes it easy to quickly connect with other singles. This Web site does not allow married people to join the database; True makes it clear that those who are married but present themselves as single are committing fraud and can be persecuted.

What you may not like about True: The number of singles on this site who are seeking a long-term relationship can be outnumbered by singles looking for casual relationships. Also, if you have a criminal record, regardless of the circumstances, you are not allowed to join.

It will quickly become evident why people don't join every available Web site — there are so many to choose from, many of which require lengthy questionnaires that can be quite time-consuming!

www.AmericanSingles.com®

The great thing about **AmericanSingles.com** is that you don't need to go through a lengthy questionnaire or even register with the Web site before you can start perusing singles in your local area. In the beginning, all you must do is input the basics: your gender, age, and zip code, as well as what you are looking for with regards to the gender, age, and location of singles. It's a very simple process to gain access to the singles database, but this quick glance will not supply you with singles that are necessarily right for you. They will simply be your preferred gender and age, and are living within the geographic area you specified.

Don't use a fake e-mail address when searching through single's databases. Sometimes sites require you to confirm your e-mail before allowing you full access to the site, and keep in mind that your e-mail address will not be displayed on your profile page in most instances.

It's possible to find out which singles are online by hitting the "Online" button. This will take you to another page where you can view the profiles of all the people who are online. From there, you can also request to chat. You will not be able to chat or contact any of these singles until you fill out the registration form. Additionally, you are only allowed a certain number of views through the catalog of available singles before you will be prompted to register with the site.

When you're ready to enter more specific information to find a potentially compatible mate, fill out the more specific form that asks about who you are and what you are looking for. You will not be able to access the singles database again until after you confirm your e-mail address through the automated system.

AmericanSingles does not offer an extensive compatibility matching system like some of the other dating Web sites online. If your goal is simply to meet singles in your area, then this can be a great Web site to use. If, on the other hand, your goal is to aggressively pursue finding the love of your life, then you will have to do a little more work with this site. You will have to decide for yourself whether the other singles within the database are compatible with you — based solely on the information they choose to share in their profiles. While this may make it more difficult to pinpoint exactly who would be a compatible match, it can also broaden your options considerably.

What's good about AmericanSingles: It's a quick process to get into the system to peruse the database of singles. This Web site also offers features for people who want to start out making friends first before jumping into dating online.

What you may not like about AmericanSingles: This site does not feature the extensive compatibility tools that some of the other dating sites have. Also, you will not be able to do much on this site until you upgrade to a paid membership.

www.JDate.com®

The very first screen on JDate prompts you to start filling out the questionnaire. Keep in mind that because this Web site is specific to Jewish people, you will be asked plenty of questions regarding your background and faith. Be prepared to answer questions regarding your synagogue attendance, whether you practice kosher eating, and which branch of Judaism you follow. It is a fairly detailed questionnaire, but you can skip the majority of the questions initially if you are anxious to start looking at the database of singles.

When you fill out the initial questionnaire, you have the option of stating that you are curious about Judaism or that you are willing to convert. It does not make much sense to post a profile on this site if you are not Jewish and you have no interest in converting to Judaism. This site is specifically designed for Jewish people to meet in the hopes of having a connection. If you are not familiar with the Jewish culture, you may not know the dynamics behind it, and the truth is that many Jewish people —just like people in other cultures — want to eventually marry someone who is like them.

If you find someone who catches your eye, you can send a "flirt" to that person's inbox. Sending a "flirt" is a quick note to a user that is meant to initiate a conversation. JDate supplies a variety of "flirts" to choose from that are supposed to break the ice and provide a safe way to prompt someone else to look at your profile and flirt back if the person finds you appealing. Members choose from a long list of prewritten flirts, like "You are my clear favorite of the un-chosen, chosen people" or "I'd travel a million miles to see your smile."

The "flirt" capability is free for the first 30 flirts, but after that, you must join the Web site by paying the membership fee. The cost of membership depends on how long you want to have access to the database and what capabilities you want to have on the site. Premium membership — which costs more than the standard membership — will put a bigger spotlight on your profile and may compel more people to check you out.

This Web site also offers instant messaging and video chatting to members. This can be a good choice if you are looking to specifically meet someone who is Jewish, but if you like the features on other Web sites better than on JDate, you can still conduct a search based on religious beliefs. The instant messaging allows you to have a real-time conversation via a text box, and opting to participate in video chatting will result in a new screen that pops up on your computer where you can see the other person while you chat online.

What's good about JDate: You can easily find Jewish singles on this site because it is geared specifically for this group. You

can further specify whether your ideal single will attend synagogue or eat kosher foods, which can be very important to
some Jewish people.

What you may not like about JDate: If you aren't Jewish, and
you don't have any plans to convert to Judaism, this site is not
for you. Additionally, you may encounter singles on this Web
site who claim to be Jewish but aren't.

www.Match.com

It's quick and easy to get started on Match.com. Unlike some
dating Web sites, there isn't a lengthy questionnaire to fill out
before gaining access to the database of singles. The only information necessary to start perusing available singles is your
e-mail address, your gender and what gender you are looking
for, the age range you prefer, and your zip code. This information takes you the singles database.

You can further refine your search by specifying what you're
looking for in regards to a potential mate's appearance, lifestyle,
religious beliefs, and other characteristics. When you find someone compelling, you can click on the profile, and you'll be asked
to fill out a more complete profile to see if you are actually considered compatible with the other person. If you're not ready
to go through the full compatibility screening, you can bypass
this option and go straight to the profile. By clicking on a profile,
you can view photos and read about the person's likes and dislikes. You can send a "wink" without paying for the service, but

you cannot e-mail the person or use the phone service offered through the Web site.

If you do sign-up and pay for Match.com, you will be eligible for the Web site's guarantee. As long as you follow the guidelines for the guarantee — such as including a photo on your profile and initiating contact with at least five other singles — then you will receive a free six-month membership if you haven't met someone special during your first five months as a member. The terms to this guarantee are always subject to change, so check out the details before signing-up.

What's good about Match.com: This site has a huge database of singles to look through. The guarantee offered by the Web site may also make you more confident when signing up for a membership.

What you may not like about Match.com: Because this is such a popular dating site, you may feel as though you are getting lost in the shuffle. Also, until you pay for a membership, your access to all the features will be quire restricted.

www.Chemistry.com®

Chemistry has one of the most interesting and fun questionnaires to fill out among all the dating sites. In addition to the usual questions about what you are looking for and what type of person you are, the questionnaire also walks the user through different timed games that are simple and fun. An example of one of these games: A line is presented to you on one side, and another line on the other side. Your job is to adjust the second line until it is the same length as the first. The site makes the claim that these games do indeed measure compatibility, although it isn't explained why. You're also asked questions that may seem a little odd, such as the length of your fingers and what type of doodles you might draw during a boring meeting. There is even a section that displays pictures of people and asks which person you would want to buy a used car from.

The questionnaire does take quite some time to finish, but it is set up in a way that makes it seem less daunting than other Web sites. Instead of filling up a page with several questions, most of the survey spans over several pages that have only one or two questions and features plenty of graphics and photos to make it visually appealing.

You can view some of your matches for free after completing the questionnaire. Chemistry has a matching system in place that categorizes your personality, categorizes other singles' personalities, then tells you why the mix of the two works well. For example, you might be labeled an "Explorer/Builder," and your match may be a "Director/Builder," which means the two of you are supposed to be compatible based on the categories Chemistry determined you both belong in.

If you decide to join Chemistry, you will be able to contact the matches that the system decides you are compatible with. You will not have access to the total database of singles, but instead will only have access to the matches assigned to you by the Web site. Unlike other online dating sites, you do not sift through a huge database of singles. Instead, you are assigned certain matches based on your "chemistry." While some people may find this restrictive, others enjoy the simplification of the process.

This site allows gay singles to register and seek out compatible singles, which is different from some of the other mainstream dating sites available online. In fact, some of the Chemistry commercials feature gay couples that have actually met through the site. For gay singles who have experienced frustration with other dating sites, Chemistry can be a welcome change.

Once in a while, this Web site offers free full-access for a short period of time, such as a free weekend worth of contacting matches without paying the membership fees. This can be a great way to get your feet wet without committing to months of membership fees. There is no set schedule published that states when these sales take place. The Web site usually advertises these specials a week or so beforehand, and sometimes television commercials announce the free weekends as they occur.

What's good about Chemistry: The matching system tells you not only about the best person for you, but also tells you more about yourself based on your answers. You may also enjoy the initial questionnaire because it is designed to be fun.

What you may not like about Chemistry: You will not have access to the full database of singles. Also, you may not like the personality labels you receive from the initial questionnaire.

www.LavaLife.com®

This Web site caters to people who want to meet someone for a potential relationship, as well as people who are simply looking for an "intimate encounter." In other words, people can log on to LavaLife and find someone local to have a one-time romantic encounter with. It's not as if this can't be accomplished on any other site for singles, but this Web site is one of the most blatant mainstream sites to promote this capability. This offers flexibility for singles to decide whether they want to meet someone for a relationship or if they want to meet someone for a shorter-term period.

You will find that many sites are most expensive if you only subscribe for one month. You will be better served — price-wise and relationship-wise — if you sign up for at least three months. However, most sites offer six-month and 12-month subscriptions. You will soon discover that the cost per month drastically decreases as you purchase more months.

You will have two choices after you begin filling out your profile: You can enter LavaLife through the main site, or through

LavaLife Intimate, which is the site devoted to intimate encounters. No matter which option you choose, after filling out a quick survey about your preferences, you'll receive a short list of potential matches. The questionnaire is not long or indepth, so the matches you receive may have nothing more in common with you than geographic location. You may also find that the matches you receive have not completely filled out their profiles. This may be because this particular Web site does not prompt users to answer very many questions when initially filling out their profiles.

If you specify that you are looking for an "intimate encounter," the process is a little different than if you are looking for a relationship. You'll be directed to LavaLife Intimate, where you will view a list of potential matches. You are much less likely to find profiles with photos available in this section, but you can peruse the profiles to find out exactly what type of sexual activities the person is interested in exploring. This section of the site is much more explicit than the relationship section, but if you are truly looking for nothing more than a sexual encounter, then this information can be useful.

You cannot contact other singles on this Web site until you pay the membership fee. LavaLife also offers a phone service where you can connect with available singles over the phone, but this service costs money beyond the membership fee because users must purchase access to the system as well as buy additional blocks of time. If you want to use this service, you can have it charged to your phone bill, or you can pay using a credit card. Some people choose to use both the phone service and the online dating services offered by LavaLife because they find people on the phone service who are not listed on the Web site.

What's good about LavaLife: This site offers a wide variety of features for different people. The singles who want to find relationships are separated from the singles who only want an intimate encounter.

What you may not like about LavaLife: People who are easily offended may have a difficult time if they stumble upon the profiles for people wanting an intimate encounter. Additionally, this site does not offer extensive compatibility services like some other sites do.

But Wait, There's More

You don't have to limit your online search to Web sites that are considered the most popular or mainstream. You may be able to find "The One" on a dating site that doesn't pay for costly national commercials or flashy Internet banners.

When searching for the love of your life online, it makes sense to check out a wide variety of options. Here is a listing of some of the less prominent — yet completely acceptable — online dating Web sites.

CASE STUDY: PAMELA'S STORY

"Growing up, it never seemed important to me to date within cultural boundaries. I mean, it was hard enough finding nice guys, let alone handsome, driven, funny, Jewish nice guys. By the time I reached my senior year in college, my religion became more important to me, and I wanted a different way to meet people aside from the bar scene, so I decided to go on **www.JDate. com**. I chose this dating site because I reasoned that if I was going to take a chance, it might as well be with people with the same religious background. I was skeptical at first, but as time went on, I grew eager to sign-on and check my mailbox. My agenda filled up fast, with sometimes several dates a week. I did come across a few weirdos, including one guy who asked me to 'rate our connection' on the first date, but I had a good experience overall. I met some nice people, got taken to nice restaurants and fun activities — including go kart racing and ice skating — and had some funny stories to share with my friends afterward. However, I never found anyone special and eventually let my monthly membership expire.

Months later, I did meet someone special on another online site: **www.Facebook com**®, of all places! I was randomly skimming through my Rabbi's friend list, spotted this cute guy, and decided to send him a little note. He ended up writing me back the longest, most sincere letter of my life. From there, we went back and forth several times a day. Brandon seemed unreal at first. While quoting his messages, my friends nicknamed him Prince Charming because he seemed too good to be true. When we transitioned to speaking on the phone, there was an instant connection. A couple weeks later, after I already felt like I knew him, we met in person. The rest is history; he is the one I want to be with forever. I wasn't looking to find my soul mate while browsing through Facebook, but it just so happened that way. Maybe it's what they say — love comes when you least expect it!"

Yahoo!™ Personals and Yahoo! Personals Premier

Yahoo! Personals **(http://personals.yahoo.com)** offers two different services: Yahoo! Personals and Yahoo! Personals Premier. Yahoo! Personals allows you to search member profiles and create a profile for free. On this site, you can receive messages from members, but in order to respond or use the messenger, you must subscribe, which costs $24.95 per month.

If you happen to be looking for a serious, committed relationship, try Yahoo! Personals Premier. The main difference between Personals and Premier is that you can take the relationship test, which helps you determine your unique love style and what you are looking for in a relationship. Premier also offers a matching system that helps its members find someone worthwhile. The rate for a membership is $39.95 per month.

You can search through the database to find potential matches based on the location and age range you are looking for. This Web site allows you to search for someone of any gender, so this is a viable option for people looking for a same-sex relationship.

Before you're prompted to register, you can view the profile of a few eligible singles, which requires a Yahoo! ID in addition to a short profile to post on the site. You won't be able to contact any matches unless you sign-up for the subscription service, but you can send "flirts" to other members with the free membership. Other members can contact you with your free membership, but in order for you to respond, you need to pay the fee.

The site is easy to navigate. It is simple to peruse the catalog of singles and read their profiles, but keep in mind that you can only peek a few times before you will be required to fill out a profile. When filling out your profile, you'll have the option to receive an e-mail newsletter full of tips for online dating. Upon completion of your profile, your information is sent in for a review to make sure that there is nothing unacceptable by Yahoo! standards, so don't fill your profile with nonsense or vulgarities — it will be deleted before anyone can view it.

> When you peruse databases of singles, pay attention to how long it has been since a person has logged on. If the person hasn't logged on for two or three weeks, it's likely you won't get a reply.

www.FriendFinder®

You can instantly access the database of singles at FriendFinder after inputting your gender, the gender of the person you are seeking, the age range you desire, and the location you want to seek within. If you want to meet people specific to your region, you can input your zip code, but if you want to broaden your options, leave the zip code blank and simply input the state you live in or the state you want to search for singles in.

You can get a small glimpse at the eligible singles who match your search criteria, but once you attempt to click on a profile, you will receive a prompt to enter more information to create a free profile. This questionnaire isn't very long and will ask you for your birth date, contact information, and specific things you are looking for in a mate such as race, religious preferences, and smoking habits. You can skip a lot of the questions on the questionnaire if you just want to get through it quickly.

You won't be able to access the database again with your username until you go to the e-mail address you provided and obtain the password sent to you. This is FriendFinder's way of making sure that you don't create a fake profile, but beware: It's also a way that this Web site gains access to your e-mail address to send you promotional offers and other e-mails.

www.Metrodate.com®

Metrodate is owned by True Communication Inc., which also owns other sites such as **www.DatingWidget.com, www. Metrofieds.com**, and **www.SearchEgg.com**. Metrodate was established in 1998 and today has more than half a million members. The site is favored by many because of its user-friendliness, outstanding customer service, and unique features.

This Web site combines online dating with local singles events. When you sign-up for a free profile, you are also signing up to receive e-mail notifications of singles events in your local area. Many members of this Web site combine their online searching with meeting people at these events.

You won't be able to see any of the photos or profiles of local singles until you complete a free profile. The information you'll need to enter is fairly simple; you can skip a lot of the questions regarding your preferences, but it's worth it to take the time to fill the profile out thoroughly if you have specific standards. For example, if you absolutely don't want to date someone who smokes cigarettes, then this is the place to make that preference clear.

After you fill out your profile, you will have to verify your e-mail address. It's not possible to simply peruse the database of singles by entering a fake e-mail address because you can't have a look without first confirming that the e-mail address you used is valid.

www.Date.com®

Date, a free online dating site, helps people find friendships, love, and romance. The site was established in 1997 and offers singles the chance to create a free profile and the opportunity to meet people from nearby or from across the globe. Date offers such features as chat rooms, Web video messaging, and audio instant messaging, and claims that most of its members are college-educated professionals living in large metropolitan areas or suburbs.

You're immediately prompted to start filling out a free profile before you can gain access to the singles registered on this site. The profile survey can actually seem a little daunting because most questions are required to have responses before you can submit the questionnaire. Additionally, when you are asked to fill out an essay about who you are and what you are looking for, there is a minimum word count. If you are the type of person who prefers brevity, this feature may make you uncomfortable. On the other hand, it is a feature that ensures all users are specific about who they are and what they are looking for. This feature can be used to your advantage because it will be easier to find profiles that aren't vague.

You can skip some of the steps, but be aware that completing the profile will result in a variety of offers. Date will want to send you e-mail newsletters and share your contact information with third parties, and it will also prompt you to download an Internet toolbar.

After you complete the profile, you can access the database of singles and look at photos and other profiles. If you find someone you would like to contact, then you will need to pay the membership fee. The fees are available in different increments: You can buy a month's worth of access, or you can buy access for a longer period of time. Keep in mind that your subscription will be automatically renewed onto your credit card upon expiration, unless you specify otherwise.

Some sites — like LavaLife, Dreammates®, Spring Networks, and CupidJunction — offer an alternative to subscriptions. Instead of paying for unlimited access for a month, three months, six months, or a year, you can purchase tokens that can be used for e-mails, chat sessions and other things. Each e-mail or chat is assigned a certain token value, and you simply feed more quarters into the machine for more time.

www.Great-Expectations.com

Great-Expectations focuses on the safety of its members and, as such, screens potential members, meets every member in person, and maintains a collection of current photos and videos that truly represent members. Great-Expectations gives its members access to a team of professionals who will help them find a meaningful relationship. The site also hosts parties and events at which you have the opportunity to meet local singles, along with a state-of-the-art matching system that will aid you in your search for love.

After filling out a quick questionnaire about your age, gender, and location, you will be referred to a local Great-Expectations office nearby. If there isn't a local office in your area, you will be invited to register for access to the online database of singles. Unless you want to travel to a Great-Expectations office, or if the nearest representative is willing to travel to your location, you will not receive the same screening and personal service that people with nearby offices receive. The online database is like other databases online for other dating sites and does not come with a Great-Expectations guarantee.

By signing up for a profile on this Web site, you're also allowing this company to share your dating profile with other sites. This company participates in a program called "Relationship Exchange," which is a system that allows dating profiles to appear on more than one site. While this is a way to broaden the audience base of available singles that can look at your profile, you should understand that this may result in your profile showing up in places that you may not want it to.

If you choose to submit an online profile, you'll find that it is a quick process, and many of the questions can be skipped if you don't want to fill them all out. After submitting the profile, you'll have access to the profiles of other singles, but pay attention to the last log-in date on these profiles — some users have not accessed the site in more than a year.

Great-Expectations has a reputation — justified or not — for being quite costly. Many consumers have filed complaints about this company, claiming that they were charged exorbitant fees and did not receive the service they expected or were promised. With a dating service that can cost literally thousands of dollars to join (depending on the membership purchased), it is no surprise that members get quite upset when they don't meet someone special. On the other hand, plenty of people were happy to pay the fees and met someone special through the service. You need to decide if the cost of the service is worth it to you, and be sure that you thoroughly read any contract you are asked to sign. Your agreement becomes a legally binding financial obligation even if you aren't happy with the results, unless you have a guarantee from the company that allows you to terminate the contract if you aren't satisfied.

This dating service is notorious for not answering questions about the actual cost of the service. There is nowhere on the site that specifies the costs of the service, and most representatives are vague about the cost until after you sit down and go through the interview process with a Great-Expectations salesperson.

Keep in mind that Great-Expectations is designed to be a one-on-one dating *service*. Although they provide Internet services, the main service involves the applicant filming a short video, which is added to a database of other videos that prospective dates can watch. While this personalized service may appeal to some people, if you are looking to get involved with online dating in the easiest way possible, then you may not like the necessity of meeting up with representatives, filming a video, and anything else that is required when using this service.

CHAPTER 4

Personal Experiences with Online Dating

One man and one woman spent a month each as members of three dating service sites:

- www.eHarmony.com

- www.Perfectmatch.com

- www.Match.com.

Here are their experiences from beginning to end.

A Woman's Experience

By Daniella Nicole

Introduction

Having been an online dater for several years, I was excited to take part in this project. I had been a paying member of Match. com and eHarmony several years prior; I was not familiar with Perfectmatch. Across the span of my online dating years, I have been a member of more than two dozen different dating sites. With most, it was only for one to six months. In all that time, there were only two that I had a membership to for more than six months.

During the time I spent on this project, I left a dating site I had been a member of for several years. I had been considering such a move before this project came along, and my experiences on the other sites I was reviewing confirmed it was the right move for me to make.

I have been involved with the singles scene to varying degrees during the years since my divorce and have dated a great deal. I have been involved in several serious relationships and was engaged at one point to someone I met through an online dating service. That relationship ended prior to our wedding day.

I have many friends, male and female, in the dating world. They vary in age, income level, religious beliefs, size, shape, background, and educational level. We communicate a great deal about our experiences as singles and as online daters. Despite the differences in who we are and in what we are each seeking, many of our experiences as singles and online daters have been similar.

My own personal experiences verify what the experts say about rejection and breakups: that the best way to look at those experiences is as a learning experience and a blessing. The blessing is in not being in a relationship that will not work or with someone not 100-percent committed to the relationship.

For some, being able to hide behind a computer screen creates a feeling of freedom to be hurtful, rude, antagonistic, or thoughtless. Going into the dating world aware of this is help-ful in developing the thick skin every single needs as he or she faces the prospect of kissing a lot of frogs before finding a prince or princess.

While I signed up with these particular sites as part of my re-search for this project, I also went in being completely hon-est about who I am and with the attitude of conducting a real search for a great match. I answered questions honestly, filled out my profiles accurately, and posted real and current photos of myself.

I did real searches based upon the things I desire most in a mate and in a relationship. I worked to find the most effective ways to use each of the sites and spent a great deal of time on each site, trying to become familiar with the features offered.

When I received new matches, I checked them out as soon as possible, and I replied to contacts as soon as I could. I only ig-nored scammers and the contacts that were truly lewd.

Juggling three active memberships was time-consuming and not something I would recommend that anyone try unless they have an awful lot of free time. There is a lot to do when you are searching, answering contacts, learning each Web site, checking out every new match, and keeping photos and pro-files updated.

I changed my profile on all three as I went in the hopes that it would help fine-tune the process. It did have an effect on the contacts I received, and it did result in some very positive remarks about my profile. Several men commented that they were impressed with my profile and the answers I gave in eHarmony's guided communication.

Continuing to fine-tune your profile, photos, and other dating site elements is crucial in the search for a great match. If you aren't getting matches or contacts you like, it could be a clue that you need to change something in your profile or photos.

With the exception of one difference that I disclose later in this chapter, I behaved on these three sites as I have and do on any other dating site. I reported scammers, closed out clear mismatches, contacted and communicated with those of interest to me, and kept my profile and photos updated.

Based upon my knowledge and online dating experience, I believe my experiences on the three reviewed sites can be considered typical. Your own personal experiences may vary.

The Signing-Up Process

For this project, I joined eHarmony, Perfectmatch, and Match. com. With each, I filled out my profile completely and uploaded multiple photos.

eHarmony and Perfectmatch both required a lengthy questionnaire be filled out before a profile was ever set up. eHarmony signed me up with my real name and gave my real first name out to my matches. Perfectmatch required a user name. I spent half an hour trying to come up with the perfect user name that was not already taken. Imagine my irritation when I discovered that even though I had to sign-up with a user name, they still gave out my real first name to matches.

Though both eHarmony and Perfectmatch require a questionnaire, eHarmony's questionnaire was significantly more detailed and more time-consuming. I spent the better part of a day signing up with all three services, including the filling out of questionnaires, filling out additional profile information, figuring out what else I had to do in order to have a complete profile, and uploading photos.

The eHarmony questionnaire did not allow me to go back to a previous page to check or change answers. It was only a potential problem for me when it came to religion, where a few religion options were listed. My specific faith was not listed in those options. I was not sure which option to click on, so I made my best guess as to how the site might categorize my particular faith. I chose correctly, as on the next page was list of other religions under the one I originally clicked, and my own faith was in that list. At that point, I was allowed the option of clicking on my correct faith as a 'sub-category' of the first option I had chosen.

Out of curiosity, I tried to click back to see what they had listed under "other," but the site would not allow me to do so. In the profiles I was sent, I noticed that many of the men of my faith whom I had been sent had made the mistake of listing our common faith under "other," and there was no further clarification. I wondered how much of a problem it was for them when it came to the matching process due to it not being clear they were members of our particular faith.

There is a way to edit a few things that affect matching, and one of them is the religion choice. By entering the "My Settings" section and then "Match Settings," the site user can make a few changes about themselves and their priorities.

Perfectmatch allows users to retake the test if they are so inclined. Though eHarmony claims they find the most honest answers are the ones given first, I think there is also something to be said for being able to go back and re-read the questions and choices to be sure they were understood and answered correctly.

On Match.com were questions to answer as well, in addition to more information to fill in to have a complete profile. This was frustrating. Though I was able to sign-up with Match.com in less time than it had taken me with the other sites, it still took more time than the average dating site.

It is exasperating to go through a long list of questions and discover that you are not even close to being done filling out your profile. All three sites were guilty of causing this frustration.

Those who don't want to spend a lot of time on the computer or Internet, as well as those who are not computer literate, may find themselves too frustrated with any of these three sites to complete registration.

Money Talks

eHarmony and Perfectmatch were the same price at $59.95 per month, while Match.com was about half the price, at $29.99 per month. All three sites offer a discount if you buy more months at once.

All offered add-ons, some free and some with a price tag. One interesting add-on with eHarmony is RelyID®. For a yearly fee of $5.95, personal identity can be verified. The RelyID logo will show up on user's profiles indicating that they have been verified as being who they say they are. A user's name, age, and location of residency get verified with RelyID.

Another purchase option was the premium version of my personality assessment results. For $9.99, the more detailed version can be purchased.

Over at Match.com were also many add-ons available for an extra charge. These options included getting mobile access to your account, using anonymous phone communication with matches, having your profile highlighted in search results, being notified when your sent mail has been read, and buying space in the first round of matches sent to new members.

All of these carried a $4.99 per month charge except for the anonymous phone communication, which was $6.99 per month.

A fun, free feature they offer is the option to add up to three testimonials from friends, family, or exes to your profile. I thought about how helpful it might be to interested men to read what other men who have dated me or been involved with me have to say. I was about to send off some testimonial requests, but I worried about how it might look to have testimonials from exes on my profile.

Non-paid memberships on all three sites are highly restrictive and pretty much useless for anything other than looking at profiles and getting communication you cannot reply to or read.

Profile Photos

Perfectmatch and Match.com have a profile and photo approval process that eHarmony does not. This results in a time delay between when you finish or update your profile and when it is published, as well as when submitted photos are posted. Many sites do require administration approval prior to profiles and photos being published on the site.

Though I do not rate compatibility by appearances and I do not want to be judged exclusively by my looks, I also am suspicious of those who do not post a photo. I have run across more than one married person on dating sites and have also run across more than one person with a criminal record. Because of the fear of being sucked in by a married person, criminal, or scammer, many are leery of communicating with those who do not have a posted photo.

Most of the people my friends and I have encountered on dating sites are not married, scammers, or criminals; however, most of those with no photo posted were indeed hiding something, and it was more often than not related to insecurity about their looks, age, or weight.

Another interesting note about photos is that most of the people, male and female, that I have met in real life do not look like their photos. They may vaguely resemble them, but many actually look better in person than they do in photos. There are some who post old or very inaccurate photos, and there are a few who look exactly like their photos.

A photographer I know once mentioned you should put very little faith into photos when judging how a person really looks. He said that lighting, poses, and other factors could all affect how a person appears in photos. Some even have their photos touched up professionally or do it themselves with programs such as Photoshop.

With my own photos, I try to have a good mix of photos so that a fair assessment can be made. Thus far, I have been recognized immediately upon sight by almost everyone who met me in real life. I have even had complete strangers approach me in real life because they recognized me from the photos they had seen online.

The Matches — Flame or Fizzle?

Though the claim is that the questionnaires are in place to help you, the user, find the most compatible matches, I did not find them to be effective for me on either eHarmony or Perfectmatch. Issues clearly addressed in the questionnaires were completely ignored in the matching process as I was routinely sent profiles of men whose own questionnaire answers were in complete contradiction to what would be compatible with me. Even things I had listed strong opposition to or that I was not interested in having in a mate were present in many of the matches. These traits and issues were clearly uncovered in their own questionnaires.

By that same token, I did not feel that any of the matches I was given on Perfectmatch or eHarmony were scammers. Most had a nicely filled out profile. I was not once contacted in any manner that I found to be offensive on either site.

Match.com is a different story, as most of the initial contacts did seem like scammers. Also on Match.com were user names that were dead giveaways as to what their true motive was – sexual flings. I did not see that type of user name on Perfectmatch or eHarmony, though eHarmony uses real names, so it is not an option there.

On a more positive note, Match.com is quick to respond to complaints about scammers and remove their accounts. Though I contacted the site about the first one, the other ones were removed before I got to the site to check the mail they had sent me. Once I checked the mail, I saw that their account had been removed. It is comforting to know that a site you are paying to be a part of is good about responding quickly to problems.

As far as matching went on Match.com, I really didn't feel like it was about compatibility. I wondered more than once if I was just sent random profiles, as they seemed to be so different from one another and did not match well with what I had answered in the questions or listed in my preferences.

eHarmony initially sent me seven matches a day, but tapered off to an average of two a day. At the end of 30 days, I had been sent more than 100 matches. Of those, about one-third had been closed either by me or by the man. Less than a dozen of the rest made any contact with me. Out of that amount, only three requested to talk with me by phone. From my own experiences over the years as on online dater, I would say those are fairly typical numbers regardless of the site. On the site I left, 100 views a month was common for me, though I did get significantly more phone and date requests on it.

Perfectmatch sent me two notices about matches, with only one match listed on each. On the site, however, I had a total of nine matches in 30 days. Out of all the matches and views from this site, I did not get one single contact — no flirts, no e-mail, not anything.

Match.com sent me notices every two to three days stating I had new matches. Each time, there were 12 men displayed on the notice. With these matches, I was allowed to change settings in order to fine-tune the process myself. On Match.com, I had accumulated more than 100 views in less than 30 days.

Most of the very first contacts on Match.com were clear "scammers," who sent out badly written form letters in barely comprehensible English. A few men sent "winks" and, when I replied, did nothing. After those initial contacts, I only received contacts from those who seemed to be "real" people.

One particular match and I exchanged multiple on-site e-mails and talked on the phone. The phone conversation was not at all what I expected from our e-mails. On the phone, he sounded like he was on drugs. He was not speaking clearly, and he could not seem to stay on any topic. Most of what he said was incomprehensible.

A few days later, he sent me a phone message and an on-site e-mail. In both he talked about how much relationships "freak him out." Most of our one and only phone conversation had comprised me asking him to repeat himself; I had never said anything about meeting or dating the man, and he was already anxious about the thoughts he was having of our future together.

Another common problem is the sheer amount of "the walking wounded" who are on online dating sites. In the online dating scene, you need to be prepared for this phenomenon.

There are many who have not done their homework, and are so lonely and in so much pain that they are looking for a quick fix. They jump quickly into relationships when they really aren't ready. I ran across a large amount of men in my age-range who had been married and divorced several times. Most of them jumped into the second and third marriages with people they met online and then claimed the person changed once they married. They had dated in real life a very short time before they married.

Many of the men I became acquainted with through this project and communicated with off-site were among the walking wounded. They admitted as much, as well. They want to be with someone, but they have deep wounds and seriously low self-esteem. Some have deep-seeded bitterness about their former spouse or partner. It becomes one more thing to screen for in the weeding-out process, and it is one thing I found that is not really addressed in the matching process.

I do not want to scare anyone away from online dating sites. They can be fun and helpful in finding a great match. However, like anything, you have to do your homework and go into it prepared. By doing so, you increase your odds for success.

Just because someone includes something on their profile

doesn't mean it's true. Sometimes it is just a matter of the person wearing rose-colored glasses about who they are. Other times it is intentional deceit. Keeping emotions out of it and taking everything with a grain of salt are two helpful strategies when weeding out matches from online dating sites.

Searching High and Low

eHarmony does not allow searching. With eHarmony, you can only select from the individuals they chose for you. This means if you desire certain criteria, and all they give you to choose from are options that turn you off, you must change what you want — or go elsewhere.

Perfectmatch allows for basic searching by age, gender, and location. There is a custom search feature that allows you to specify searching for items you have previously listed in your preferences. This raises the question as to why you would need to use these things in your own searches if they are presumably included in the matches the site gives you. Would you not come up with the same results? That seemed a little redundant and confusing to me. The third method of searching on Perfectmatch is by the letters from the personality assessment.

One really fun aspect of Match.com searching is that it shows profiles that are similar to the one you are checking out. This is a helpful tool for when you find a profile that really catches your interest. You can then find more profiles like the one you are currently viewing, and you will have a better chance of finding a good match out of those choices.

Another fun search feature is MatchWords™, which is the Match. com name for keyword searches. It is a feature that sometimes requires approval from the site administration during use. The only keyword I had to get approval on, though, was "sci-fi."

I used words that described me as well as words that described my interests. You are allowed up to 50 MatchWords, though I made less than a dozen. I figured most of the words people would search for would be flooded with results, and the unique ones I came up with might not get searched at all. I opted to stick with the basics I had covered in my profile.

How is Compatibility Defined?

Though sites that match by "compatibility" claim personality and personal values are more important than appearance, they do push members to upload photos. eHarmony offers an option for closing matches due to no photos being posted.

As with height, eHarmony claimed body build was not a compatibility factor, but lifestyle and activity levels were. I remember very specific questions about my own lifestyle and activity level. A high percentage of the matches I was sent also were completely incompatible with me due to lifestyle/activity level. Needless to say, I was not impressed with the eHarmony matching system and felt the questionnaire was a complete waste of time considering the matches I was sent.

That does not mean I was not sent profiles of some really good men — I was. I just did not get the level of matching I expected from the advertisements for the site and from how in-depth the questionnaire was.

At Perfectmatch, the matches seemed to be a little better as far as actually matching me, though they were much fewer in number than I had been given at eHarmony and at Match. com. By the end of the 30 days at Perfectmatch, I had decided that the site was really more of a "searching" site than it was a "matching" site. They offered more search features than the other two sites, and they gave me far fewer matches.

Slow and Steady Wins the Race

Though eHarmony now offers a method for speeding up the communication process called "Fast Track," almost all of the matches I was sent indicated they preferred the "guided communication" process. I found that interesting considering the high number of men I know who routinely complain about women moving too slowly when it comes to making phone calls, exchanging phone numbers, and going on dates. I have no clue as to why there is such a disparity between the profile settings I saw on matches from eHarmony and the preferences of the many single men I know in real life. Perhaps many men missed the option to change the setting to Fast Track when signing up.

There was no real action to report from Perfectmatch, but on

Match.com the contacts were good about writing e-mail and fit into the average time range I have experienced when it came to asking if they could call me or if I would call them.

Does eHarmony Work?

I have an acquaintance from another site who found her match on eHarmony, and there are plenty of testimonials listed on the site. I also know several people who were notified by eHarmony that no match was available for them at that time.

I was sent many matches, and I believe at least some of the weeding-out process was taken care of for me by the compatibility questionnaire. That being said, I noted that a few very obvious incompatibilities were not filtered out. I think the programming can stand a little fine-tuning.

There is no search feature, so you are locked into choosing from among only those they send you. It then becomes a system of rating who you like best from the group you were sent to select from.

There is no way to tell at a glance who is a paid member and who is not, so if you are ignored or, if a match initiates no action, you don't know if the reason is because they are not a paid member and can't communicate with you — or if they just are not interested.

I personally know many singles that are on more than one site, and of those, they only have a paid subscription to one or two. With the cost of eHarmony, it is likely that fair amounts of matches received are people who are not paid members and therefore cannot communicate with you. This frustrates the process even further as, again, you can only choose from among those they send you.

Adding the anonymous phone call feature was one of the best things I think they did. This service allows people to talk to each other via phone without actually knowing the phone number of who they are talking to, as the transfer goes through eHarmony. When you sign-up for membership, you are asked if you want to participate in Secure Call. If you do, you input your phone number(s).

When the call shows up on a phone screen or caller ID, it is listed as unknown, thus those who screen calls may miss it. A permission request will come through via e-mail first, so recipients can approve them and be aware that a call will be incoming at some later time. If you miss the call, a segment of a message will be left on your voicemail. This is your clue that the unknown call you missed may have been the eHarmony call you approved.

Guided communication and the phone calls allow users to become acquainted before agreeing to spend the time and money involved in meeting in person. Many matches may have to travel significant distance to meet, so having this safety net is a plus.

When you get a closing, you can send a final message, which are pre-written messages such as wishes for good luck and requests for another consideration. When I received closings, I just closed out my side of the match with no final message.

Does Perfectmatch Work?

Of the three sites I tried for this project, I was the most disappointed in Perfectmatch. The best way to sum up the site is that if eHarmony and Match.com mated, Perfectmatch would be their offspring.

The lengthy questionnaire was not as detailed or as long as the one from eHarmony, and it was used in their matching system. There is a deal breaker section that allows you to add some criteria for your matches such as ethnicity, location, and age range, which you can freely change. They also allowed for searches.

One of the first things that annoyed me with Perfectmatch were the sales pitches. At sign-up, they push other features, such as books, to help you find your match. In mail from the site, I was given only two matches — and a slew of sales pitches.

On the site, I had a grand total of nine matches, and of those, five had no photo posted. The site really pushed the search features and advice by means of a book you could purchase from their expert, Dr. Pepper Schwartz.

Like eHarmony, once you fill in the basics and get through the questionnaire, you are not close to being done with setting up your online profile. I found this to be the least user-friendly site of the three, and I was not at all impressed with this site, though they have plenty of testimonials and also allow for searching.

Perfectmatch continued to frustrate me across the board with how it was set up and how difficult it was for an advanced user like me to learn. I cannot imagine someone less computer literate having an easy time with sufficiently using this site.

Though I had problems with the matching system of eHarmony, by far it was more enjoyable, straightforward, and user-friendly. There were not nearly as many extra items to set up in my profile, and eHarmony did not spam me with promotions. In contrast, e-mail from Perfectmatch was almost entirely spam.

My experience with online dating sites is that numbers matter. The more views and matches you receive, the better your odds for getting contact. The more contact you get, the better your odds for actually making it to the dating stage where you can really discern if someone is a true match or not. Having low numbers on Perfectmatch hurt me a great deal in this regard. Though I took initiative on all the sites, it did not pay off on Perfectmatch.

There are success stories from Perfectmatch. I am sure there are people who love it and who would have success there. For whatever reason, it just didn't work for me, and it was not a site I found to be helpful or fun to use.

Does Match.com Work?

Match.com is pretty much your standard online dating site. They have improved the site a lot since I was last a member, but I think it is more likely to attract those looking for casual connections than those seeking a real and lasting relationship. Many sites online offer most of the same features and are less costly or even free; furthermore, some of the extras Match.com charges for are free features on other sites. If you added all the extras onto your membership, you could easily be paying about the same amount per month for Match.com as you would for eHarmony or Perfectmatch.

Match.com had something about **www.Chemistry.com** on their site that initially looked to me to be some kind of matching test or extra feature. All too late, I realized it was an additional dating site. I started receiving a lot of spam from Chemistry after I joined Match.com, but I do not know if it is from joining Match.com — or if Chemistry kept my e-mail address after I deleted what I started there.

What works for Match.com is the site administration's vigilance about removing scammers and its lack of ads, which free sites have to use in order to get revenue. Another thing that works for Match.com is being able to find similar profiles so easily, which makes searching a fun and easy process. Keyword searches can be fun and interesting. It is amazing what results you can get from using interesting and unique words in your keyword searches.

Though there were a lot of profiles, I doubt they all were paid members looking for a relationship. The scammers I was contacted by initially illustrate to me that Match.com is being targeted by them. Some of my friends make it a game to do searches and out the scammers to the administration of dating sites. Match.com is the most vigilant about removing scammers of all the sites I have been on.

A nice part of Match.com is that when you view a profile, you can see at a glance how you match up with someone based on a chart on the profile, which indicates with a green button how you match up on different criteria.

Of them all, I felt like I had the most freedom and the most fun on Match.com, though I had more contacts on eHarmony.

And the Winner is . . .

If you are really seeking a relationship, a place like eHarmony or Perfectmatch might be a better place to check than Match.com, which is more conducive to casual dating.

All three had on-site relationship advice and tips for online matching. All three had their own relationship expert on board. And all three had success stories and a high number of members.

But I got the most matches and the most action from eHarmony and Match.com. I had the most fun playing with features on Match.com, but eHarmony seemed to me to be the most user-friendly. With all three sites, I was immediately given matches and immediately received views. On eHarmony and Match.com, I also immediately started gaining contacts.

eHarmony required the most time to sign-up with and was expensive to join on a month-to-month basis. Match.com required the shortest amount of time to sign-up with and was the least expensive of the three to join, unless you buy all the add-ons. Then, it is about the same price per month.

I became acquainted with some really nice men from two of the sites, and though I am not a success story for any of the sites, I do think online dating sites can work; I know too many people in real life who have found their mates through such services to say otherwise. I have made many great friends and have been able to date some fantastic men from being a member of the online dating world.

Based upon my own experiences, I believe that if you are considering joining an online dating site, you should plan to be there for at least six months in order to really get a feel for it and to get to know the people there. Buying memberships in larger lots such as six months at sign-up gives you a discount and allows you to have a low-cost, month-by-month renewal after the purchased term runs out.

If I absolutely had to select one of the three sites, I could easily eliminate Perfectmatch. Deciding between the other two would be difficult, as they both have pros and cons in areas that matter to me. If cost was not considered, I might pick eHarmony, as it did seem to do some weeding out for me. I did not feel that the matches from Match.com were selected in any relevant way. I think I fared better in my own searches and with the men who searched for me. On the other hand, I liked being able to search for my own matches and to find similar profiles quickly.

eHarmony allowed me to make instant changes to my photos and profile, while Match.com required site administration approval first. eHarmony offers free anonymous phone calls, while Match.com charges a monthly fee for the service.

If money and time were not factors, I would choose both. By using both, I would feel like I would be getting a good selection and have plenty of opportunities to conduct my own searching and fine-tuning in the process. Neither was a better match for me than the other.

A Man's Experience

By John Peragine

When I began this experiment in Internet dating, I thought that it would be a breeze. I had seen so many commercials about online dating services that I was really curious about it. I had my ups and downs through the process, but it was definitely an eye-opener. All of my thoughts and beliefs about online dating were shattered, and it was a very sobering and educational experience. I chose three services in which to explore this 21st century form of dating – eHarmony, Match.com, and Perfectmatch. I signed-up for each service for one month to learn the ropes.

eHarmony

My beginning was logging onto the site for eHarmony. As I looked at the home page, I knew immediately that this site was going to be unique in its structure and offerings. On the page are two options — single and married. The single tab is the dating Web site in which they claim to have helped millions of people find love, and the married tab is for those already married, designed to help people strengthen their commitments. It struck me as a way to dissuade married men or women from straying, which I think is brilliant.

I chose the single side. When I was trying to begin the log-on process, though, the site consistently crashed on my Firefox® Internet browser. I could not get it to load and had to resort to opening the site in my Microsoft® Internet Explorer® browser instead. After I logged in and filled out the questionnaire, I had no further problems with Firefox.

The log-on began innocently enough, asking for a first name and other basic information. As I progressed to the second and third pages, things began to get a little more personal.

By the third page of questions, the questions related to aspects like my physical attributes and ethnicity, and it was at this point that the rating scales began. These scales ranged from one to seven, allowing me to rate the importance of certain attributes in my search for a date.

In the next few pages, the rating questions continued, this time regarding my personal interests. These rating scales are used to match people together, and the more closely people rate certain things and rate their importance of attributes in a partner, the more likely the computer will match them together.

There were also true or false questions concerning my personality, which did not leave too much variety in my answers. This section was followed by my living skills, in which I picked three answers from a large list. I found this limiting and not very accurate. In all of these rating scales, I could never explain my answer or expound on it; it was all based upon numbers.

eHarmony also featured a page or two asking about my drinking and smoking habits, followed by questions about attributes I would look for in a match. The entire process took about 20 minutes with its relatively slow-pitched questions and did not delve into any really sensitive areas. Also, there were not many sexual questions at all. I noticed that because I am a male, the site automatically assumed I was seeking a woman, and if I were a woman, I was seeking a man. This is obviously a heterosexual site.

One of the questions asked early-on was regarding religious preference. All of the major religions were listed, as well as a spiritual/non-religious option. Later on, I realized that this was one of the first things that can be seen when looking at a person's profile.

After answering the questions, I was prompted to upload a picture, which I did quite easily. I could have stopped here. eHarmony has a non-paying membership to their site, though it is extremely limited. At this point, the site would only allow me to send "ice breaker lines," which are short, one-line messages that you can send to those you are interested in. Some say things as simple as "Hi," though there other short messages that comment on pictures and profiles. Most of them request communicating with the person. The ice breakers are limited to one per match, so after the initial contact, you must communicate in a different way.

If I wanted to do more than send people ice breakers, I needed to pay for a membership. I picked the one-month option at one payment of $59.95. With a membership, all those questions were compiled into a report that could be accessed from the front page. It seemed as if a computer calculated numbers and compiled a standard report for my particular results.

The report was broken down into different sections: Introduction to Agreeableness, You Are Best Described As, Words That Describe You, A General Description of How You Interact with Others, Negative Reactions Others May Have Toward You, and Positive Responses Others May Have Toward You. This seemed like a great psychological profile, as it was mostly correct — but not totally. The computation was done by a computer, so there was no one to discuss my answers with. It was rather cumbersome to read, and if I had any notion to read other's profiles to the detail that was offered, I think I would give up rather quickly. The system does not allow you to go back and change your answers; you would have to start from the beginning again to open up a new account.

At this point, the site was pretty easy to navigate. It let me know what my current matches were and at what status my communication was with them. Everyone on the site is listed by age and first name; no last names are ever displayed, neither a phone number, nor a complete address. However, the profiles do show what city and state the users live in.

On my homepage were four other tabs: My Settings, About Me, My Matches, and My Report. The "My Matches" section explained in more depth about matches that the computer had made for me and what the status was with other matches I was in communication with. The "About Me" page contained simple and quick information like my age, height, and location. This was the information most people see when they first view me as a match. I could also add additional information about myself, including books I have read, hobbies, little-known facts, and my "Must-Haves," and "Can't Stands". Under these sections were a number of statements and I had to pick 10 of each.

Here, I could upload more pictures. eHarmony allows for each user to upload a maximum of 12 pictures, though I kept it simple and left only two pictures. Also under this page was the option of RelyID, which verifies your name, age, and city for $5.95 a year.

Finally, the "My Settings" tab allows you to customize how you interact through eHarmony, letting you control what people see and what types of communication you are interested in. One of the settings is the "Preferred Communication Type," which really sets eHarmony apart from other services. You have two options: Guided Communication and Fast Track. Fast Track is the open-communication option allowing you to view matches, send e-mails and communicate directly with users right away. I chose the Guided Communication. While this process seemed well-planned, it could appear frustrating and intimidating to many.

If you are interested in someone or the computer matches you with someone, the site allows different stages of communication, which I had to navigate through to talk to someone. However, I could skip these stages if I chose and if a potential match agreed, at which point the communication would go to the Fast Track. The steps were:

♥ Read her About Me

♥ Send 1st Questions

♥ Read her Answers

♥ Answer her Questions

- ♥ Read her Must Haves and Can't Stands

- ♥ Send Must Haves and Can't Stands

- ♥ Answer her Questions

- ♥ Send 2nd Questions

- ♥ Read her Answers

- ♥ Read Dr. Warren's Message

- ♥ Start Open Communication

There was a list of questions that I could choose from, and I could pick only five. I chose to send the same five questions to every potential match, then I would have to answer my match's questions. It was like a long, drawn-out game of chess. The problem for me: It is difficult to get to know someone through lists and pre-fabricated questions.

At the end of the exchange of questions was Dr. Warren's message. Dr Warren is the creator of eHarmony and the spokesperson who is often seen on commercials on television. His message talked about the best way to approach a match and also discussed safety.

When I got to open communication, the e-mails that were sent went through the eHarmony system, with an anonymous e-mail address created by the system. There are many fail safes on the system, as at any time, a person could choose to quit communicating — and that would be the end of it. The only way a person could continue to communicate is if I gave them my personal e-mail address or other personal information.

So what happens when a person wants to talk to the person on the phone rather than e-mail? eHarmony has this covered by offering a secure online phone. It costs an addition $5.95 a month, but you can talk to matches through an anonymous system without any worry of long-distance charges.

I ended up with about five matches per a day. If a person does not want to proceed further after seeing your picture and reading your profile, he or she has the option of putting the communication on hold — or terminating it.

My feelings were actually becoming a little hurt, as I was barely getting a nibble. I put my actual picture up and wrote honest statements in the "About Me" section. I began to realize a couple of things as time passed: eHarmony and the other online dating services that I tried all seemed to have the same pattern of pursuit. The men were chasing the women. I had to pursue matches because most of the women did not; they waited for men to contact them.

So I tried an experiment. I changed my picture to a picture of a man I found on the Internet who most women might find attractive. He was young and in tip-top condition. The result of my experiment was an influx of requests to communicate from women of all ages and backgrounds.

Overall, though, I had a few communications with women on eHarmony. It was labor intensive because of the guided communication; conversations that could have taken place in minutes turned into days and weeks. Also, it took practice to figure out all the different options and levels of communication.

Of the three sites, eHarmony seemed the most professional and planned out. There were a number of e-mails that encouraged me to extend my membership after I canceled. Realize that if you do not enter your profile and cancel your membership, the site will continue to renew it every month and charge your account. When I did cancel, sales reps called me a number of times to try to get me to sign back up, and they also asked for reasons why I canceled.

Match.com

Match.com jumps right into the creation of a profile. This was different from eHarmony; in fact, just after I filled out my profile, I was able to look for matches.

After my profile was completed, I was directed toward a set of questions that began with general information items and information such as, "What is your sign?" and "Do you have tattoos?" This was a much different experience than eHarmony. These questions required me to type out my answers rather than answer with rating scales like with eHarmony, although it was a bit harder to navigate here. The site did have a few questions that I could click and pick the answer in a multiple-choice fashion.

Match.com also asked questions about children and, overall, the questions were more probing than eHarmony. There were also questions about my ethics, the languages I speak, and my ethnicity. There were even questions about my family, such as information about any brothers and sisters that I may have.

The questions turned toward what I was looking for in a mate, beginning with what I thought was physically attractive and even a question about how much money my match needed to make. After this step was complete, I could add a headline to accompany my profile. Mine read, "Looking for Fun and Excitement." I was able to also upload my photo, which was a simple, quick process.

I was all ready, except that all I could really do was "wink" at people, a quick method of letting someone know you find them interesting. They are notified and have the option of winking back; if they are a paid member, they can respond to you with an e-mail.

I signed up for the monthly rate of $34.99, and there were many other options that I could add on such as:

Matchmobile: This service costs $4.99 a month and sends messages to your mobile device when the system finds a match for you or someone is trying to contact you.

MatchTalk: This is similar to the service that eHarmony offers in that it allows to you talk to someone anonymously for the rate of $6.99 a month.

E-mail Read Notification: This service notifies you when the other party has read your e-mail. This costs $4.99 a month.

Highlighted Profile: This option changes the color of your profile and makes it stand out amongst the rest. The cost is $4.99 a month.

First Impressions: This ensures that potential matches receive your profile first by e-mail when they sign-on. This service costs $4.99 a month.

You can also chose a package deal that includes a number of these services. All of these charges are in addition to the base monthly price.

Match.com is so confident about their services that if you do not connect with someone in six months, they will offer another six months free. They also offer a link to their free online magazine called *Happen*, which offers dating tips.

Once I was able to sift through all of these decisions, I decided to stick with the basic one-month service. At first, responses were slow, but it picked up a little, as I sent out about five winks a day to new possible matches. Just like with eHarmony, I received daily notifications that I had new matches to look at, based upon my geographic location. When a match was made by the computer system, we both had the opportunity to communicate, through winks, instant message, or e-mail. There was the fourth option of talking on the phone, but I needed the extra paid service to access that.

I had some luck with the wink option, garnering some matches who either winked back or sent an e-mail. Yet most of them just never responded. I did send a few e-mails to the matches and received maybe 10 percent or less of a response there. I also tried the instant messaging feature, which involved a pop-up box, but I never received a response to instant messaging.

I also experimented with my picture on Match.com as I did with eHarmony, and I even used the same attractive male stranger's picture. The result was more queries from women wanting to chat. I began to get a regular influx of winks and short messages. When I tried to return a message from a match, I often received a message that they no longer had a profile, and so I had no way to follow-up. I had many matches try to get me to communicate with them off the site — to no avail. If you try to type your e-mail in a message, it will automatically change it to the anonymous Match.com address. Therefore, you can only communicate through their site.

Another feature on my profile was MatchWords, which are

words that someone searching can pick up on when searching manually for a match. As I viewed profiles and sent messages, the system would send me a set of three similar matches I might be interested in. The problem with this is that they could be anywhere in the world, as these suggested matches were due to words in profiles rather than geographical closeness.

With this site, I can view who has looked at my profile, and there is also a page called "My Connections." Under this section, I can view all my matches. One of the items of interest is the "Who Favorited Me," a list of favorite matches of each member. I was lucky enough to be placed on one person's favorite list. The bad news is that they never answered my e-mail.

Here are my stats on Match.com after a month:

- ♥ **Viewed Me**: 52

- ♥ **Winks**: 12

- ♥ **E-mails Received**: 21

- ♥ **E-mails Sent**: 24

- ♥ **Favorites**: 1

- ♥ **Connections (matches)**: 36

Perfectmatch.com

The last site I tried out was Perfectmatch. It began much like the others, with general information like my e-mail address and gender. The next few questions were about my physical appearance and race. The sets of questions began to feel a lot like eHarmony; this time, however, there were only two possible answers — true or false.

The first section dealt with my values and ideals and asked about topics such as my feelings about sharing religious traditions and my views on politics. There were also sections requiring a few different choices from lists, and the next section of questions asked about "deal breakers," which are items that I either could not live with or not live without in a relationship, such as whether a match was a smoker or a workaholic.

This was followed by many separate sections filled with questions about love and lifestyle, personal energy, decision-making abilities, and other personality traits.

In true online personality test style, the system created an organized report, complete with a pie chart. A paragraph described what type of person I was with sets of words, like "high energy" and "optimistic."

At the bottom of this brief report were words that described my optimum mate, like "risk averse" and "high energy."

These are the words the system uses to try to locate matches for me. In my case, the whole process required $59.95, with a buy-one-month, get-one-month-free offer. This was similar to Match.com. Perfectmatch does offer a six-month rate, but this is not mentioned right away. When I logged on later, there were offers to upgrade my membership.

When comparing all of these services, I realized that all of the systems that were in place served a few different purposes. First, they allowed me to explore different possible matches by checking out their profiles and sending some questions before I committed to talking to them. This allowed me to sift through those I might be interested in and those I did not want to pursue.

Another service this provides is safety. You can be anonymous for as long as you wish, and should you choose to break off communication, there is no way users could continue to pursue you, unless you purposely gave them more personal contact information.

Perfectmatch seemed easy to navigate. It could be the simplicity of their options, or that I had become a pro at online dating by the time I began communication through Perfectmatch.

On my page, I had various tabs to select from, and was able upload pictures to my profile rather easily. My profile had all of my basic information and the answers from my questionnaires that I took when I first logged on. They were separated into the following areas:

♥ Values and Ideals

♥ Duet Analysis

♥ In My Words

♥ My Photos

Perfectmatch also allowed me to change and edit everything I chose, including all of the answers in the Values and Ideals section, as well as the analysis. I really liked this feature because on eHarmony, there did not seem to be a way to change my answers on the personality profile.

I sent a number of "ice breakers" on the Perfectmatch system and only received one reply. I received about four matches per day, but none of them ever sent me an ice breaker, which come in two levels. The first set contains innocuous questions to begin a dialogue. The second set is much more personal. The system tracks which ice breakers are being used and who they are being used with for quick reference.

The other nice feature is that I can manually change what the system considers a match. In the Duet analysis, I mentioned the words that I would be a good match for. Under my profile, I can change any of these words to something else. This feature seems unique to the Perfectmatch system.

In addition, I do not have to wait for the system to make matches for me. On Perfectmatch, I had three searching options. The first was a quick search in which I filled out a few fields to find women quickly. There was also a keyword search that looked for certain words in their profiles. Finally, there was a custom search in which I could search any part of people's profiles for certain answers, such as those looking only for Muslim women who were nonsmokers. These searching options allowed me to search for possible mates without waiting, and I could even save the criteria that I was searching for the next time I logged on.

One of the newest functions available on Perfectmatch is the "Compare Us" utility, which places my profile next to the profile of the person I am interested, in side-by-side. This allows comparison of our answers and compatibility all on one page.

The Perfectmatch site also offers an e-mail inbox that works like most other e-mail systems, letting me even block unwanted e-mails from particular users if I wished. The ability to communicate on this system openly was much easier and quicker than on the other two sites I tried out.

How I Fared

I took a solid month to try out these three services. As I traversed these systems, a pattern of women became evident.

More than 80 percent of the women were divorced. Of these divorced women, more than 90 percent of them were recently divorced. Another interesting statistic is that most of them had children under the age of 18 living with them.

Also, many of the women I met were middle-class to upper-middle class professional women. Many had college degrees. Many of the women I found were nonsmokers who drank occasionally. These were not only the women I was matched with, but these were women who generally turned up in searches I made of on all of the dating sites.

I did not meet any women who made me fall in love with them instantly and swept me off my feet. There were many interesting women I met with whom I could definitely be friends, based on our common interests. These sites helped me find potential best friends, but I never felt that any of them would be romantic matches.

Even though I set my settings on meeting any women, I was consistently matched with Caucasian women. Of the non-white women who were matches, I only had two African-Americans, one Asian, and two Hispanic women. I was only matched outside my religious preference twice, and that was on Match.com.

I was curious about this, so I looked at many different women on these sites. I found that there were plenty of different races represented, but for some reason, I was never matched with them.

I admit that I cleared out the profiles that I was not physically attracted to first before looking at any profiles. I was not too interested in the survey analysis or multiple choice answers that women gave; I was more interested in their introduction or handwritten descriptions of themselves and what they were looking for. Also, I looked at their religion, interests, and hobbies. As I went through each stage, I was able to sort out more matches. This may seem methodical in a way, but I believe that it served a purpose.

In some ways, it was like speed-dating. I could cut through all the small talk and see if I would be vaguely interested in someone. If I was not, then I did not have to engage that person any further. I may have just looked them over and moved past them.

Of the three sites, I only communicated with people from eHarmony and Match.com. It was not for lack of trying on Perfectmatch, but no one seemed interested in getting past the first set of ice breakers. I have chosen two people, one from eHarmony and one from Match.com, to talk about. Names have been changed.

Suzie Q

I met Suzie on Match.com. I sent a wink to her, and she began with an e-mail response. Immediately, she seemed aggressive in her response as she asked me whether I meant to wink at her or not. As we communicated, we tried to find commonalities such as where we had lived, or if maybe we knew the same people.

The process turned dark as there seemed to be the impression that I was looking for a Barbie doll and not a real person. I ended the communication quickly after that. I sent about 21 e-mails and received 24 over a three-week time period.

Bonnie B

This was a totally different experience. We went through the necessary communication levels and finally got to open communication on eHarmony. This process seemed to take forever, though, and I did not feel like I knew her any better going through it. There were questions that I wanted ask but could not until I reached the stage of open communication.

Once we were able to have open communication, we talked about commonalities, and she seemed interested in me. It was through this type of communication that I felt that I had found a good friend — but not a soul mate. She eventually did find someone she was romantically interested in, and we ceased communication.

I never got to the point of talking about phone calls or off-site communication. Part of it was that there just was not enough time after all of the back-and-forth questions. The other thing I noticed was that many people used online dating because they did not have time for real dating. However, this lack of time also made it difficult to have *any* type of relationship. At the rate I was going, it would be months before I could find the right person who had time not only to communicate, but to meet in real life.

I mentioned earlier that most of the women I encountered were single mothers, many of them with careers. So between going to work and taking care of their children, there was not a lot of time left to meet someone, let alone go out on a real date. Even if they wanted to, they had to figure what to do with their children. Online dating seemed like a good solution for many of these women, as most of them e-mailed me late at night after everyone was asleep and they had time for themselves.

While using these services, if you become tired of talking to someone, you can just chose to talk to someone else; you don't need to make any kind of commitment. Online dating services help you socialize in a society in which you run all day and end up busy at night, as well.

At the end of this experimental journey, I said goodbye to these three dating sites. When I finally decided to close my membership on eHarmony, it took me through at least three pages that were not easy to navigate before I was sure that my account was closed. In fact, I ended up at the beginning a couple of times because the choices of what button to click were confusing. Each page asked me to reconsider and gave me relationship advice, taking the tone that real dating could be dangerous, and that I was safer using eHarmony. I mentioned earlier that I had to stop recurring payments and that I received phone calls asking me to reconsider. The site even offered discounts if I reactivated my account.

The next service I closed my account with was Match.com. I had to search far and wide to find the right page to close my membership, which ended up being under my account status. There was an extra step to actually hide my account and stop people from sending me e-mails. I did get a confirmation by e-mail that my membership was canceled; a couple of days later, I received e-mails trying to get me to reactivate it.

At the bottom of my account settings, in small letters, was the link to close my account for Perfectmatch. They offered me another free week to reconsider, but I declined. I did receive an e-mail confirmation of my cancellation, as well as a phone call. The representatives were pleasant, but I was firm that I did not want any free weeks.

Each of these services offered something different, and I hope that my experiences can help you choose the right site for your needs. Each had their own strengths and weaknesses. You can try out each of these sites for free, but with limited functioning. Make sure you take the time to choose the right one before investing a lot of money. All three sites I tested use questions to gather enough information to help match you with the right person, but this can be a hit-or-miss process. It will not do the important work for you, which is to get to know the person and determine if they are the one for you. Just like dating in the real world, it takes time and effort, and while the preliminary work of finding potential matches is done for you, you must commit some time and effort to follow up on those leads.

CHAPTER 5

Social Networking Sites

S ocial networking is a great way for people to stay in touch, but it's also evolved into a method for users to meet new people. If you haven't yet used social networking Web sites like **www.MySpace.com**® and **www.facebook.com**, then you may not be familiar with the potential usefulness of these sites.

In social networking, users obtain a free Web site within the network. These sites are usually referred to as "profiles" and are somewhat similar to profiles listed on dating sites. You can post a photo of yourself, list your likes and dislikes, and search through other profiles based on gender, location, and similar interests.

Plenty of social networking Web site users maintain pages as a way to stay connected to friends, family, and colleagues. Users can post updates of their current status, such as their moods and what they are doing. For example, MySpace allows users to choose among several smileys to indicate how they are feeling, while Facebook prompts users to declare what is on their minds. When you open people's profiles on either site, you can also see if they are online (unless the users have blocked this feature) and initiate an instant message conversation that allows you to chat in real time.

How can you use these general social networking Web sites to meet other singles? These sites can be great for meeting other singles in your area who may not be actively looking on other Web sites for a date, and this can certainly work to your advantage. After all, an unsolicited message from a potential date can be especially flattering to someone who isn't active within the online dating community. Most social networking Web sites also offer chat rooms and other features designed specifically for users who are looking to meet someone new.

What is the best thing about social networking Web sites? The answer is simple: They usually don't cost a dime to join.

www.MySpace.com

MySpace is a social networking site that allows members to interact with their friends' friends. The site is entirely free and allows members to share photos, blogs, and interests with a community of millions.

You can use MySpace to talk to people online, find someone to date, play matchmaker, and more. The site allows you to conduct a search using basic search criteria and offers its own instant-messaging service as well.

Getting Started with MySpace

Signing up for MySpace is easy and quick. You don't need a profile to start sifting through other people's profiles, but keep in mind that some people set their profiles to "private." This means you won't be able to access their site until you have created your own profile and have sent a "friend" request that must be accepted.

You don't need to know someone personally to become a user's friend, on MySpace or any other social networking site. In these instances, a "friend" is someone who has sent a request to someone else to acknowledge a relationship. If you aren't familiar with social networking, then you will quickly learn that the term "friend" is used very loosely on these sites. While some people only accept "friends" who are true, personal friends, other people collect "friends" without much thought, or to make them appear popular.

Because every user individually sets the privacy and security settings for his or her own profiles, you will likely encounter many different situations on MySpace. While some users allow everyone on the Web full access to their profiles, other people will only accept friend requests from people who know their last names or e-mail addresses. If you are using MySpace with the intent of meeting someone new, then you might want to set your security settings as loosely as possible; otherwise, there won't be very many potential dates who can view your profile or send you a message. On the other hand, don't get too relaxed with your security settings and privacy. Don't create a profile that is accessible by everyone that publicly lists your phone number, address, and workplace.

MySpace has a few different features that allow you to meet other singles. You can search for people based on gender, location, interests, schools they have attended, and careers. This means that if you want to use MySpace to find people who live nearby, enjoy the same books you do, and work in a similar field as you do, you just need to select this information and MySpace will return suitable results to you. MySpace also features a classified ad section where singles can connect, with sections for women seeking men, men seeking women, men seeking men, and women seeking women. Furthermore, the chat function on MySpace makes it easy to quickly connect with people after you initially review their profiles and decide that you are interested in learning more.

There is also a function on MySpace that allows you to browse through the profiles of people according to criteria you set, including marital status, age, whether the profiles feature photos, and other qualifying factors that can make it easier to find people who may be compatible with you. Make sure that you have filled out all this information in your own profile, including what you are looking for — dating, networking, or friends

— so that other singles can find your profile by conducting a search.

If you want to use MySpace in the capacity of a dating site, be sure to make your profile visible to everyone, post presentable pictures of yourself on the site, and list yourself as "single." This will ensure that your profile shows up when someone conducts a search for singles.

Facebook

Facebook is another social networking site that allows members to connect with friends and co-workers. The site lets you find friends or dates, keep in contact with friends, upload as many photos as you want, and share your favorite links and videos. Facebook is free to join; all you need is an e-mail address. The site boasts advanced privacy features that allow only your friends or people in your regional network to view your profile, if you wish.

Getting Started with Facebook

Facebook offers an ease of use that makes it simple to get started Unlike MySpace, you won't be required to list your academic or professional affiliation, but instead will only need to supply a valid e-mail address.

Facebook is not designed to be a place for singles to meet other singles, but it can certainly serve as a method for connecting with people. You may find that profiles are more restricted on

Facebook than on MySpace — although this is not always the case — because the general population of users is somewhat different than those using MySpace, as Facebook has its origins in universities and thus typically appeals more to an educated, older crowd. However, both sites have a large variety of people as members.

After you create your Facebook page, you can look through other profiles within your network (the geographic group assigned to you by Facebook based on the zip code you enter) and beyond. You will not have access to every single profile because of individual security settings. If you want to allow other people to contact you, be sure to set your security settings to where anyone can view your profile and contact you.

You can also filter your search by looking at other networks of people or by searching according to academic affiliation. Because not everyone supplies this information, it may not be a completely reliable way to find someone from a specific school. For example, if you want to meet someone who attends the local university, you can search based on people who claim the university as their school. Not everyone registers an affiliation, so this method certainly isn't foolproof, but it is one way you can be selective about which profiles you take the time to look at. It's easy to contact someone; simply send a message or "poke" the person, which is the Facebook equivalent to a quick hello.

Other Social Networking Sites

Although MySpace and Facebook are the two most popular social networking Web sites available on the Internet, there are plenty of other sites that are more specific to certain populations. Many dating Web sites offer social networking capabilities including forums, instant messaging and blogs, but you may be able to meet someone interesting using a social networking Web site that is designed for school alumni or professional associations. For example, if you would really like to meet a lawyer, go to the Web site for a professional association of lawyers and see if there is a social networking forum available on the site. It is certainly a roundabout way to meet someone online, but it's an option nonetheless.

New social networking Web sites are popping up all the time. Look for a social networking Web site that is designed with your hobbies or passions in mind. Here is a brief list of some social networking Web sites that you may want to have a look at to see if the site appeals to you, and better yet, if there are any members on the site who appeal to you:

♥ AsianTown.net   ♥ Buzznet®.com

♥ AllHealthcare.com   ♥ Classmates®.com

♥ BlackPlanet.com®   ♥ CollegeTonightInc.com

♥ Bebo®.com   ♥ DeviantArt®.com

- ♥ ElfTown.com
- ♥ Flixster®.com
- ♥ Flickr®.com
- ♥ Friendster®.com
- ♥ Fubar®.com
- ♥ GamerDNA™.com
- ♥ GoodReads.com
- ♥ Hi5™.com
- ♥ LinkedIn®.com
- ♥ LiveJournal®.com
- ♥ MyChurch.com
- ♥ MyLife.com

- ♥ NetLog™.com
- ♥ PerfSpot.com®
- ♥ Orkut®.com
- ♥ OutEverywhere.com
- ♥ SocialVibe®.com
- ♥ Tagged®.com
- ♥ Twitter™.com
- ♥ UrbanChat.com
- ♥ VampireFreaks.com
- ♥ Yuku®.com
- ♥ Zorpia.com

The sites listed above are some of the highest-ranked social networking Web sites. Rest assured that even those sites that are not designed for singles to meet still cater to this goal by allowing people to meet and chat on the site. The best way to get started is to find a social networking site that appeals to you and join. If you like online gaming, join GamerDNA; if you are a fan of photography, go to Flickr; and if you want a site that is specifically for dating, check out Fubar. Many Web sites that don't have social networking capability yet might soon add this feature because it is so popular — so check out sites that you already frequent to see if you can join a social network there.

A Quick Glance

Here is a quick rundown of some spotlighted Web sites according to what type of Web site it is. Use this reference when looking for particular features on a Web site, specifically, whether the site offers comprehensive matching services or if, instead, the matches are based solely on aspects such as gender, age, and location.

While some people enjoy the matches that come from compatibility sites, others would prefer to use their own best judgment.

Compatibility Sites

These Web sites use various scientifically endorsed methods to ascertain the compatibility of members:

- **Perfectmatch.com**

- **eHarmony.com**

- **JDate.com**

- Chemistry.com

Database Free-for-Alls

These Web sites allow you to specify what you are looking for in a potential mate, but do not require (or do not offer) compatibility tools:

- True.com

- AmericanSingles.com

- LavaLife.com

- Personals.Yahoo.com

- Match.com

- FriendFinder.com

- MetroDate.com

- Great-Expectations.com

Dating Sites for Same-Sex Relationships

Some of the dating sites offering heterosexual relationships also cater to same-sex relationships. Here is a brief listing of some of the best Web sites offering matching specifically for gay or lesbian people:

- Gay.com

- GayFriendFinder.com

- PrideDating.com®

A Sampling of Sites

If the Web sites listed above don't interest you, check out some of the other popular Web sites listed below. If you still don't find a Web site that perks your interest, then rest assured there are plenty of other dating sites available online. Conduct a simple Internet search to find more dating Web sites to suit your taste.

♥ Animalattraction.com®   ♥ Craigslist®.org

♥ Animalpeople.com   ♥ Cupidjunction.com

♥ Asianfriendfinder.com   ♥ Datemeister.com

♥ Bookofmatches.com®   ♥ Datemypet.com®

♥ Catholicmingle.com   ♥ Datingdirect.com

♥ Christiancafe.com™   ♥ Drdating.com

♥ Christiansingles.com   ♥ Dreammates®.com

♥ Collegeluv®.com   ♥ Epersonals.com

♥ Connectingsingles.   ♥ Equestriansingles.com
  com

- ♥ Facelink™.com
- ♥ Farmersonly®.com
- ♥ Friendsearch.com
- ♥ Ge-dating.com
- ♥ Greatboyfriends®.com
- ♥ Greensingles.com
- ♥ Hurrydate™.com
- ♥ Iwantu.com
- ♥ Jmatch.com
- ♥ Jumpdates.com
- ♥ Kiss.com™
- ♥ Kizmeet.com™
- ♥ Loveaccess™.com
- ♥ Lovecity.com™
- ♥ Matchmaker.com®
- ♥ Matchwise.com

- ♥ Meetup®.com
- ♥ MegaFriends.com
- ♥ MillionairemMatch. com™
- ♥ Millionairemate.com
- ♥ Mingles.com™
- ♥ Mustlovepets.com
- ♥ Mycountrymatch. com®
- ♥ Nerve®.com
- ♥ Okcupid®.com
- ♥ Oneandonly.com
- ♥ Overthirtysingles.com
- ♥ Passion.com®
- ♥ Personals.com®
- ♥ Planetout™.com
- ♥ Plentyoffish®.com

- ♥ Sciconnect.com
- ♥ Seniorcircle.com
- ♥ Singleparentmeet.com
- ♥ Singlesnet®.com
- ♥ Soulmatch®.com
- ♥ Spiritualsingles.com
- ♥ Sugardaddie.com®
- ♥ Thesquare.com
- ♥ Ucandate.com
- ♥ Udate.com™
- ♥ VeggieCommunity.
  org
- ♥ Usamatch®.com
- ♥ Veggiedate.org
- ♥ Veggiefishing.com

- ♥ VisionPersonals.com
- ♥ Wealthymen.com

CASE STUDY: NANCY'S STORY

"Jeff contacted me first through Love@AOL personals. I looked at his profile and the cocky, beer-in-hand photo that he had posted and thought, 'This guy's a player.' But we exchanged e-mails for a while, and he seemed nice and intelligent. So we e-mailed back and forth a couple of weeks. Then, he sends me a message that he feels he needs to be honest, that he 'might have met someone,' but he would still like to keep in touch as friends if that was all right with me. Still thinking he was a player, I thought, why not? So I e-mailed back that, sure, we could still be friends. His e-mail in response was basically, 'Oh, I'm so glad, because I got stood up.'

I think it was shortly after that when we finally met in person for dinner at Olive Garden. Both of us were late. I think it was about 7:45 when I got there, and he'd been waiting for me for just a few minutes. He admitted to being relieved that my profile picture was a real one. We stayed out talking until about 3:00 a.m., and I never went out with anyone else again.

It was the end of January when we first met. By the first week of June, I was pregnant. I moved in with him over the summer. He proposed the following January, and we were married February 1. Seven years and two kids later, we're still going strong. "

CHAPTER 6

Crafting the Perfect Profile

When it comes right down to it, you will probably find that nothing matters as much as a great profile when it comes to attracting the right people. A great profile matters more than which dating site you join because most singles perusing databases won't make an effort to contact someone who doesn't have an intriguing profile.

A profile doesn't have to be mysterious to be intriguing. On the contrary, you want to make sure to give an accurate representation of who you are because, otherwise, you're not really telling the truth. The question is this: How do you create a profile that is not only accurate, but also compels other singles to contact you or to respond to you when you contact them? There is a definite art to creating a great profile, with many aspects like your photo, tagline, and the information you present about your likes and dislikes, hobbies, and any other pertinent information you add to your profile. How do you know when you're saying too much or too little? How do you decide which picture to use on your profile page? How do you present delicate information in a way that spins it into a positive attribute instead of making people skip your profile after reading the first few lines?

Don't underestimate the importance of a great profile. Singles searching through databases online may not spend very much time on a single profile unless something grabs their attention. After all, there are so many profiles to look through and so many different sites to explore that it simply isn't feasible to assume that people can spend a great deal of time reading before deciding whether to pursue the person or go on to the next profile. For this reason, your objective when creating your online dating profile is to grab people's attention and *keep* their attention. Keep in mind how people read online content: Instead of reading each and every word, they usually skim through to grab the important points and maybe go back to read everything in its entirety if they feel compelled to do so. Instead of writing a novella regarding your life's experiences, you want to come up with a way to present your best attributes to people as well as give them a good idea of what you are looking for.

The very first thing you need to think about is your profile picture. Your profile picture is incredibly important. Don't even entertain the idea of putting up an online profile if you're not willing to put a recent picture of yourself on the profile as well.

If you don't put a photo on your profile, then you are effectively eliminating a good portion of possible responses. Simply put, most people won't even bother to look at a profile if there is not a picture attached. There are a few different reasons for this, but perhaps the most important is that people seeking a personal connection will automatically feel distant when looking at a profile without a picture. A profile without a photo seems incomplete and perhaps a little shady; it makes people wonder what you are trying to hide. Are you horribly unattractive? Are you much older or younger than you claim to be? Do you not have any recent photos because you're in jail, or you haven't figured out how to use a digital camera? These aren't the kind of questions you want people asking themselves when they are looking at your profile for the first time.

Now that you know that you need an online profile picture, how do you know what kind of picture to place on your profile?

EXPERT ADVICE: NICOLE SETTLE OF COLE SETTLE PHOTOGRAPHY

If you don't have personal access to a professional photographer to give you advice regarding the best way to get a great profile picture, use this information from Nicole Settle, a professional photographer who is well-versed in making people look their best in photographs.

Show Your Personality

I'm one for never showing too much. With that said, if you're really outgoing, you might want to rein it in a little for a portrait. Don't look like a Mentos® commercial! Don't try to fake a smile; it always looks fake. Some people don't do well with the thought of trying to look at a camera and with not obsessing about all the horrible pictures of their past. If you tend to hate your portraits, give your camera to a trusted friend and have them snap off some candid pictures of you in your element. Use your own camera because if you know that you are the only one who will decide and edit your pictures, it's easier to endure it and not think about some picture of you that you hate ending up on someone's Facebook or MySpace page for the whole world to see.

If you are going to use props, don't overdo it. You'll end up looking like a high school drama student if you pose with a funky hat, cane, and feather boa. If you are crazy about your cat, maybe have the cat on your lap, but don't do the cheesy hold-the-cat-up-to-the-camera and imitate-their-expression pose, complete with big eyes and pouting lips; it's cute for children and elderly women, but for the average person it just doesn't work. If you want anything in the photo besides yourself, make sure that it is only supporting you, not taking the focus in the picture.

Getting a Great Profile Photo

Try to keep your chin level with your shoulders. People tend to angle their chins down in a photo and this only causes double chin or loss of detail in the picture. If you keep your chin level, or even slightly higher, you will be much happier with your photos.

Clothing is an interesting obstacle for a photographer. Having people show up for a shoot in T-shirts that have writing or graphics on them can be frustrating. Graphics and texts usually only distract from the photo — not to mention, if you prefer black-and-white photos, graphics or stripes can make the viewer dizzy, which, again, takes away from the focus of the photo — you. A good rule for picture day is to wear solid colors and don't forget to be comfortable. If you are trying to wear clothing that is unnatural for you, it will

EXPERT ADVICE: NICOLE SETTLE OF COLE SETTLE PHOTOGRAPHY

show in the pictures. If your everyday clothing preference is jeans and a T-shirt, wear it! Just be sure the T-shirt is a solid color with no writing on it.

Lighting is a photographer's best friend and elusive enemy. I prefer to take photos outside. The best times to do this are when the sun is not at full intensity, such as early morning and late afternoon. If you try to take a portrait when the sun is at full intensity, you will squint into the sun no matter where you stand. For the best photos, you want slight shadows on your face to show depth and shape; try taking a photo under partial shade and in full sunlight and you'll see the results for yourself. Natural light is always beneficial to a photo. If you have nothing but a window and a point-and-shoot camera, you can still get a well-lit portrait without expensive lighting equipment. If you don't know how to use lighting, stick with natural light. The less forced a picture is, the better the result will be.

Keep it Real

Photoshop® and similar programs can be useful tools if you know how to use them and understand the boundaries of reality. For example, if you have acne that you would like to soften or remove, using Photoshop to achieve this will still produce a fairly close representation of you. But if you try to change your eye color, take off some weight, and modify some features, you will wind up looking fake. You will be losing the entire purpose of creating a portrait, which is to show who you are, not how technology and a few mouse clicks can make you appear to be. Remember, less is more, and less is also more believable.

If overly altered, and if you're new to Photoshop, the changes to a photo can be easily spotted. Usually, the person's skin is unnaturally smooth. Everyone has wrinkles. Softening them can usually go unnoticed, but if you remove them completely, you'll wind up looking like an alien.

How can you tell if someone else has altered their profile picture to make them look better? Look for slight wrinkles around the eyes and on the forehead — this is natural, and if they are missing, then the photo has probably been altered. Another dead giveaway is awkward edges. If someone is removing part of their face (like a double chin), the normally complete and smooth edges will be usually be ragged or incomplete.

CASE STUDY: JOHN'S STORY

"I left for the Air Force in 1994, but I didn't return to Michigan until 2006, at which time I was divorced and unsure of what I really wanted in a partner. I was dating a lady long-distance with whom I'd previously been involved with, and one day, she asked me about what I was looking for in a long-term partner. I was raised in a Catholic family, but my faith had not been important to me growing up, and it wasn't until I divorced that it started to become important to me again. When I told the lady that becoming Catholic, or at least considering it, was part of my criteria, she ended the relationship. She then gave me some of the best advice I've ever received: 'You need to seek somebody with common interests.' It sounds so simple, but how easy is it to join a site for laughs or looking for somebody when you aren't even sure of what you want? Too easy.

I took the easy route — and her advice — and went straight to **www.CatholicMatch.com**, where shortly after joining the site and making some e-connections, I happened across a profile that I really liked and said 'I'd like to meet her.' OK, yes, I saw her picture first and said that, but honestly, everything about her said that she was the lady I'd been looking for to be my wife. As luck would have it, Annie was not only open to relocating, but also attracted to my strong desire to raise a family deeply rooted in Catholicism.

This has all happened between June 2006 and now. I met Annie online February 2007 and I proposed on July 9, 2008. We are getting married this summer. We have yet to send our story in to CatholicMatch, but we will at least send them a blurb because everybody likes a happy ending."

EXPERT ADVICE: TODD C. DARNOLD, PHD.

Dr. Darnold is a business professor with Creighton University. He uses his education and training in business and marketing to create an analogy between marketing a business and marketing yourself in the online dating world. Just as businesses must make their product appear appealing and useful to target markets, people delving into the world of online dating must figure out how to make themselves as appealing as possible to their target audience: a compatible date.

Recruiting Models

There are two ways to approach recruiting people. You can go with the model where you build up all your best attributes, overemphasizing them sometimes to the point of borderline dishonesty. The alternative model is what we call the Realistic Job Preview Model, where everything is completely up-front and the idea is to find the best fit. This model is much better in terms of long-term relationships. The first tends to rely more on inducing positive affect and impression management. One can only "impression manage" so long before it hurts the relationship.

You can brand yourself up front if you're just looking for a short-term thing. Over the long run, however, if you haven't been real, there won't be any fit going forward. If you haven't been given the opportunity to actually find *true* fit, on values, beliefs, personality, or whatever it might be, in the long-term, you're doomed. If you're going to "brand" yourself, so to speak, are you going to brand yourself using realistic cues or are you going to brand yourself using positive affect and present yourself in a way that would be good for the short-term?

Accentuate the Positive

Businesses try to paint a holistic picture, such as "We don't pay above market, but we invest a lot of that money in benefits" or "Our work schedule is more flexible." The other way to think about it is you want to make sure you sell with your strengths, just so those strengths are accurate if you're going to take that approach. What is it about you that is really positive? Build your "brand" around those two or three things, downplay or don't mention the negatives. As long as the two or three things that are really important about you are out there, that should be enough cues for another person to interact with you. Even if it is online, people can see that they should be a fit on at least two to three core attributes.

EXPERT ADVICE: TODD C. DARNOLD, PHD.

There is a lot of evidence to suggest that beyond two or three core values, we don't actually cognitively process the specific things we are looking for. Zero in on two or three things that you find especially important and then put the whole picture together around those things that fit with you. We tend to overlook some things because we want to, in a sense, "correct the triangle." *We want to make sure that everything aligns, so if the big stuff is there, we'll gloss over the stuff that doesn't matter as much or actually figure out how to make it seem good.* Your core attributes are going to drive your decision-making, and you will be most happy when your core values are aligned.

Looking for a Good Fit

If you haven't found a profile that looks like they authentically focus on those core attributes that you're looking for, it probably doesn't make a lot of sense to reply based on other factors, such as because the profile picture is cute. If you're looking for something long term, that probably isn't what you should be doing. On the other hand, it is a goal-driven process. For example, if your goal here is to meet a bunch of people and have fun, then different rules apply. At that point, you're looking for different things.

Talk about your strengths and core values. If you really know your core values, then just explaining, illustrating, and giving examples of those core values or activities should be the best advertisement you can give to the person you're trying to find.

Revealing Your Negatives

The worst thing businesses can do is pretend like there aren't any problems — because that's just phony. On the one hand, a company may be laying off massive amounts of people in one group, but then in another group they might have to hire like crazy. You need to explain away the issue and say, "*This* is who I am as a person, even though I'm caught up in this other thing, but that will be taken care of by x, y, and z. I'm working my way through it, and this is what I've learned about relationships."

There are going to be risks in every situation, but as long as people are trying to learn from their mistakes, hopefully people are going to give us a little grace.

EXPERT ADVICE: LORI GORSHOW, MSW
"THE DATING COACH" OF *DATING MADE SIMPLE*

Gorshow is a professional dating coach and online advice columnist who specializes in assisting people with navigating the dating scene. Her professional experience extends to helping singles craft the very best online dating profile, as well as how to respond to communication with other online singles.

Appeal to Your Target Audience

When you're writing an online profile, there are things that you should start thinking about even before the writing process begins. You want your writing to appeal to your target audience, so, if you're a woman looking for a man, you want to write in a way that appeals to men. If you're a man looking for a woman, you want to write in a way that appeals to women. If you have any question about it, ask people who are in your social circle who are members of the opposite sex to review your profile.

The most important thing is to write for your targeted audience. The second most important thing is to write to attract the kind of person you are looking for. Don't describe yourself in a way that won't attract the personalities you're looking for. If you're looking for somebody who is sensitive, then you shouldn't have a tone within your profile that's tough. Don't write to appeal to everyone; write to appeal to who you're looking for.

You will also want to write distinctly. When you think about writing distinctly, a good profile length is between 200 and 275 words. It shouldn't be less than 200, and it should never be more than 275. If it's too short, it won't provide enough information. You want to answer three broad-based questions:

1. What am I like?

2. What are my interests?

3. What am I looking for?

When you're thinking about the first question, consider your personal philosophy or your personal values surrounding family, friends, and work. You want to present a well-rounded image of you.

"What am I into?" is not into the past tense, or what you would be into if you were with the right person. Rather, how do you spend your time *right now*?

You're marketing yourself. You want to think about leading with your strengths. When you're writing, you really want to present that image of yourself to the

EXPERT ADVICE: LORI GORSHOW, MSW
"THE DATING COACH" OF *DATING MADE SIMPLE*

reader. "I'm not coming with baggage; I left my suitcase at the door, so you don't have to worry about that."

Rules for Crafting Your Profile

In your profile, don't use words that are absolute, like "never" or "always."

When you're on a general site that is not designed to cater to a specific audience, you want to think that the reason you're there is to cast a wide net. You want to get people's attention. For example, suppose you have some health issues where you've been on medication. Don't put that in there unless you're on a site specifically for people with similar issues.

Let's say that you lost your job or you're in school and working to better yourself; that's a positive reframe to "I work as a waitress." Or, if you just got laid off, don't put that in your profile. Instead, say, "I'm in transition."

For example, if you have been out of work for a year, what are you going to do to manage yourself? "I do volunteer work" or "I've been taking courses" or whatever else you have been doing should be included in your profile.

You will want to hold some things back initially because it creates a mystery about you. You want to convey enough information for interest, but you also want to work toward that face-to-face meeting because then people get to get to see all of you. There should be a sense of mystery about you. Give information, but not too much specific detail in the very beginning.

In some cases, you want to be able to put specific information into your profile because it limits the people you can be with. For example, if you have an allergy to animals, then you might mention it in your profile. "I love pets, but I suffer from allergies, so I'm looking for a person who has an animal that doesn't shed," or something that addresses the specific issue because otherwise you may get someone who has a cat or dog with a lot of hair.

Using Specific Dating Sites for Specific Types

If you're a smoker but you're working on kicking the habit, you might put that in your profile. You want to avoid opinions that aren't generally accepted by other people like, "A woman's place is in the home," "Republicans are old-fashioned," "I'm into being green about everything," or "I'm a vegetarian and absolutely would never go out with somebody who eats meat or wears leather."

EXPERT ADVICE: LORI GORSHOW, MSW
"THE DATING COACH" OF *DATING MADE SIMPLE*

Unless you're on a site that is specifically geared toward these lifestyles, try to avoid absolutes.

The Importance of Photos

About four to five photos within your profile are good. When you're putting your profile online, one of the things that you want to think about is that initial opening picture. Remember who your audience is. That opening profile photo is important. It's also important to know that if you don't have a picture, you won't get looked at by about 80 percent of the singles online.

The purpose of the photo is to show you in the best possible light, doing things that you enjoy or in places that you enjoy. You really want to present confidence and show that you're relaxed. You want the photos to be clear and sharp. You want to be the center of the photo. So, while the mountains or ocean behind you may look great, the person is looking at *you*.

Whenever you take yourself out of the photo, or it's not clear, it gives an impression of trying to hide something. Photos should be recent. You want to make sure that your photo does not show that you cropped somebody else out of the picture. Don't allow someone else's hands to show in the photo. There are services that can eliminate a person in a photo for you; if you really want to use that particular photo, pay for the service to get the person removed from the shot.

Don't post any photos with you and your kids, or you and other people. If you love dogs, horses, or another animal, then that's an OK photo. Using a photo of you in a group of people means that a person has to figure out which person is you. If anyone in the photo looks similar to you, then people may not be able to tell which person within the photo is actually you. You don't want to set yourself up — or set someone else up — to be disappointed. Ideally, an online dating profile photo should only feature you.

Don't use photos of you in a bathing suit, shirtless, or in revealing clothes. While you are not trying to convey the image that you're a prude or standoffish, you also don't want to use sex appeal as an advertisement. A sexy photo of you can attract someone of a different type of mentality. Remember: Who do you want to attract? Do you want to attract someone who is looking specifically for sex, or do you want to attract someone who is intelligent, has a professional job, and is personable and pleasant? A person looking at your profile photo has limited information on you; if everything you wear is too revealing in your photos,

EXPERT ADVICE: LORI GORSHOW, MSW
"THE DATING COACH" OF *DATING MADE SIMPLE*

then an opinion is formed of you that may not be indicative of who you really are. Clothes should not be too tight, nor should they be too big.

Writing for our Target Audience

When you're writing to attract a woman, manners are really important, but not the kind of manners that make you appear wishy-washy. Include a bit of assertiveness as well. Women will respond to that because it is an attractive quality. A sense of humor is effective. Energy is attractive. Don't imply that you're dating for fun or that you are just seeking out friendships. Don't imply that you had a negative experience with women and now you don't trust them. Don't write that friends are *everything* to you or, worse yet, that your mom is everything to you.

Women should try to come across as fun and interesting. You need to demonstrate a balance. Don't focus too much on your children or on your baggage. Don't fill your profile with specific details of exactly the kind of man who should contact you or who shouldn't respond.

People are naturally attracted to those who feel good about themselves. In general, write in the present tense. You may love long walks on the beaches at sunset, but do you live in a state where you get to do that?

Taglines

Your tagline should relate to you, present the positive, and show something about your interests. A great way to think about taglines is considering them as online license plates. Try to use alliteration if you can. For example, "Long Lean Lady" sounds better than "Skinny Tall Blonde."

Don't use your actual name for your tagline. One of the worst ideas is to make your tagline nothing more than a shortened version of your name followed by your birth month, day, and year.

If you are given the option to also write a subject line, do it. You should look at your subject line as your second opportunity to grab someone's attention. Write something that shows your humor. You can also write something that's interesting or something that you're passionate about. You don't want to be too sexy or romantic or over-the-top in any way. Don't write things like "I'm looking for a husband" or "I want my soul mate." Instead, think along the lines of "Active guy with great sense of humor who loves to laugh," "Tennis player seeks partner for a game of doubles," or even "Bring your ABCs: Adventurous, Brave, and

Charming." You want it to be six to 12 words because that is enough to grab somebody's attention.

Paying Someone to Write Your Profile

There are a few services that write online dating profiles for a fee, but you can also get this service from someone who does marketing or freelance writing. Ask questions before hiring someone. How will you get a sense of who I am and how will you convey that? What if I'm not happy with what you write? There should be some kind of guarantee of satisfaction. Ask for testimonials or information about people who are happy with the service they provided. If you're using a company that is advertising online, be sure to ask for some samples of their writing so you can get a sense of their style. Ask for some creativity in the writing.

Listen to how they describe what they are going to do to get to know you and to individualize it for you. Someone you pay to write your profile should talk to you quite a bit. It doesn't have to be in person —you can speak on the phone — but the person should gain a sense of who you are. The person you pay to write your profile should present you in the best possible light.

The cost of using a professional service to write your online dating profile ranges anywhere from around $30 to more than $100. In general, the more of a guarantee the service offers and the more individualized the profile, the higher the cost. You may want to get a couple of different profiles written so your profile on eHarmony doesn't look like the one on Match.com. If you have the exact same profile on several different sites, it may give a prospective match pause.

Being Safe When Creating Your Profile

Don't give personal information on your profile that would allow someone to find you in person. When writing your profile, you really want to think about not giving anything that can specifically lead someone to you, like your job title or the names of your children.

Some people list their astrological sign because that's something that they're really into, but be careful to not give your personal birth date on your profile because you don't want somebody to steal your identity with your information. Some online dating services will do background checks of members, but some do not. If not, you can do your own personal background check as long as you have the person's name. For example, if you have the other person's first and

EXPERT ADVICE: LORI GORSHOW, MSW
"THE DATING COACH" OF *DATING MADE SIMPLE*

last name, it's very likely that you can Google that information to pull up at least a street address.

If you give someone your home phone number, it is likely that he or she can use that to track down your address. If you have a weird feeling about one of your prospective dates, know that you can go into public records and put in the person's name to see if there is any legal or court actions against the person. You can find out if the person has been involved in a crime; this type of information can come up by exploring government records and putting somebody's name in. Someone who is just getting back into dating and may not be savvy enough to take all of the hidden cues that are coming their way should utilize these methods.

Contacting Other Members

Always personalize the message you're sending to someone else. You want to spellcheck your notes and make sure that you have the right name for the right profile. It can be very embarrassing to send a note to someone else with the

You may have to check a box when filling out an online dating profile so that your birth date is not listed for everyone to see.

wrong name. You should also try to be specific about something in the other person's profile that stood out. You want to tell the other person what it was that attracted you to the profile. You want to say something that shows that you actually read the profile as well as the impression that the profile gave you. When you're writing, the first paragraph is your chance to let the other person know what attracted you to the profile. Let the person know what it was that caught your attention.

The second component is to say something about you. You may want to put something in there that is about you, your philosophy, your interests, and something that relates and connects to the person you are writing to. Keep it brief, but let the person know how to get in contact with you.

EXPERT ADVICE: LORI GORSHOW, MSW
"THE DATING COACH" OF *DATING MADE SIMPLE*

Sample First Contact

Hello_____,

What attracted me to your profile (beyond your obvious great smile) was your introduction. I was intrigued with *"I am a very passionate person – so everything I do, I do it with energy and love."* After reading this, I knew I wanted to meet the woman who is not afraid to take a risk and jumps into life with her heart wide open. Not only did I think you must be incredibly brave, I also thought you a kindred spirit. You have a great ability to express who you are and what you want clearly, succinctly, and with confidence. Your confidence is striking and attractive.

Something about me…I love to stay busy, but this is balanced by making time for family, friends, and giving back to my community. I enjoy the outdoors and going up to the mountains for fun, sport, or a change of pace. I also love to travel nationally and internationally. Traveling gives me an opportunity to meet new people and see new sights. A belief…you can tell more about a person based on what he/she does and not by relying on what the person says he does. To find out if I am worth my salt, you're going to need to respond to this e-mail.

I am intrigued by what I have read about you and would like to learn more. Check out my profile, and if you like what you're reading, let me know. I look forward to hearing back from you.

Sample Second Contact

Hello ____

If you checked out my profile or read my previous e-mail, then you know me as _____. I'd like to take this opportunity to be less formal, so let me introduce myself. My name is _____. I get that online dating has its pluses and minuses. It can be difficult to separate the good guys from the jerks. So on my own behalf, I can assure you that I am worth responding to. I'm one of the good ones — the kind of guy who opens the door for a woman, calls when he says he will, and is not afraid to go after what he likes.

Life is too short to have regrets, and not responding to this e-mail request might just be one of those regrets you'll wish you had acted on. So take a second look at a guy who should be your first choice.

Talk to you soon…_____

CHAPTER 7

Creating Your Own "Rules"

One thing that most dating experts agree on is that you need to know what you are looking for before you actually start looking for someone to date. Instead of simply logging on to dating Web sites and browsing to find someone "interesting," you should have a relatively good idea of what you are looking for in a potential mate. Create a set of rules that — although somewhat flexible — signify what you need and what you will not accept. The reason these rules need to be somewhat flexible is that sometimes people aren't entirely sure of what they will absolutely not accept and what they absolutely need until they meet the love of their life.

Composing Your List

It is worth it to sit down and take a hard look at what you want in a potential mate. Don't wait until you're filling out an online profile to make these important decisions because you might find yourself overwhelmed with the entire process and unwilling to reflect on these important details.

Ask yourself these questions before you start actively looking for singles online:

- ♥ What do I want in a mate?

  - o Do you want someone who has the same religious beliefs and values as you?

  - o Do you want someone who enjoys the same hobbies as you?

  - o Do you want someone who works within a certain profession or has a certain level of education?

  - o Do you want someone who is similar in age to you?

  - o Do you want someone who has children?

- ♥ What will you *not* accept in a mate?

  - o Are there certain religious or spiritual beliefs that you cannot accept?

  - o Does your mate have to be within a certain age range?

  - o Are there physical attributes that you will not accept, such as over or underweight?

- o Are there certain ethnicities that you will not date?

- o Are there geographic restrictions to where a potential date should live?

- o Are you willing to date someone who drinks alcohol or smokes?

- o Are there certain hobbies, such as video games or hunting, that you will not accept?

When you are making a list of your rules for potential online dates, it's important to keep in mind that you are creating a list of the things you really want, not a list of things you want other people to believe you want. In other words, if you know without a shadow of a doubt that there are certain people you would never want to date, then this is something you need to acknowledge and make clear on your dating questionnaire. This doesn't mean that you need to place within your profile that people with these certain traits need not apply, but rather that it's something you should specify when filling out the initial questionnaire if you are given the option of marking certain traits as either acceptable or not acceptable. The same applies for any other things that you will or will not accept. Most initial questionnaires on dating sites allow you to disqualify potential matches based on religious beliefs, geographic locations, education level, income, smoking habits, and a wide variety of other aspects that can be important predictors of how compatible you may be with someone.

But you should want to keep your options open and be somewhat flexible with the rules you create for yourself. The truth is that you never know what you may find yourself attracted to. You may *think* that the love of your life will be a certain height, working in a certain job, attending a certain church, and engaging in certain activities, but once you start sifting through all the available singles online, it may become obvious that you are ready to broaden your horizons.

This can be especially true for people who have not had much exposure to cultures and locations other than their own. They may naturally assume that they want someone like the people they are already familiar with, but, once they have a look around, it suddenly dawns on them that there is more out there than what they are used to.

But this is not to say that if you are an avid churchgoer that you should entertain the idea of meeting someone whose online dating profile denounces all forms of organized religion, or if you are an animal rights activist, you shouldn't force yourself to be open to date someone who hunts as a hobby. Don't compromise your own beliefs to fit the mold of what other online daters are looking for. On the other hand, the rules you create for yourself should not be based on superficial things that don't really define who you are.

When you are composing your list of rules for what you are looking for and what you won't accept in a potential date, limit the items to things that are fundamental to a person. Don't expect a person who hates organized religion to suddenly want to attend church with you as a result of dating you, and don't think that the hunter will decide to go vegan in an attempt to woo you. In the unlikely event that these huge changes take place, what are the odds that they will stick? After all, when people make lifestyle changes for another person (instead of for themselves), there is a good chance that they will eventually revert to their original behavior.

In other words, a change made to impress someone else is unlikely to be a permanent change.

What does all this mean for your online dating profile? It means that you should go into online dating knowing what you are looking for and what you absolutely will not accept. It also means that you should keep your options flexible when it comes to the rules you make that aren't real deal-breakers. Be flexible, but at the same time realize when there are certain things that you simply aren't willing to be flexible about.

Try not to exclude things that you don't have experience with. You may think that dating someone who has children is something that you could never do, but that may be because you have a false expectation for what a single parent will be like. You may be sure that you could never fall in love with a person who never attended college, but if you are constantly surrounded by highly educated people, you may have an unrealistic view of what a person without a degree is like. Don't allow your preconceived notions to greatly limit your search for someone online.

Reading Profiles

After you have figured out what you want — and what you don't want — how can you make sure that the people you contact through online dating have the attributes you are looking for? To ensure you aren't wasting your time on potential dates that will never be right for you, one of the most important things you can do is to thoroughly read the profiles of people before you initiate contact or respond to a contact request.

In the beginning, it may be tempting to jump right in and enthusiastically contact every profile with an attractive photo or promptly respond to every single communication you receive from another online dater. This is especially true if you are new to online dating and haven't been on the dating scene for a while. The problem with the tactic of blanketing the Internet with profile responses is that it can be compared to walking through a singles bar and stopping to talk to every person there.

You need to have some qualifications for what you will accept in a potential date and what you won't accept. Blindly responding to every profile or composing a response to everyone who contacts you doesn't make any sense, especially after you spent the time to write your list of what you're looking for and what you won't accept. Why go to all that trouble if you are just going to contact every somewhat-attractive person within your desired geographic location?

There are a few different reasons why you should always read an online profile before you initiate contact or respond to a communication request.

Make Sure the Person Qualifies

You will increase your odds of meeting someone you are compatible with if you don't simply judge photos or seek out clever taglines, but instead remember the things that you know you are looking for in a person. You will also know when you must automatically disqualify someone, even if the person has a great smile or writes well.

First impressions on an online dating site are different from first impressions with face-to-face meetings. A photo and an online profile can give only a mere glimpse at what a person may actually be like. By thoroughly reading through a person's profile *before* you initiate contact, you will have a better idea of what you may be in store for with that person. If your needs and dislikes are pretty straightforward — such as wanting someone who has the same religious beliefs as you and not wanting to date someone who drinks alcohol more than a couple times a week — then you can find what you are looking for within the body of a person's profile. After all, the profiles are there for a reason; they are an important tool, and you should take advantage of the information that is readily available to you.

Remember: Not all online dating sites prescreen people for you based on compatibility and what you are looking for. If you are using a Web site that does nothing more than grant you access to a database of singles based on your geographic location, then you'll have to read through the profiles yourself to weed out anyone who isn't suitable.

Make Yourself More Attractive

When you first initiate contact with someone, one of the surest ways to guarantee that you won't get a reply is to send an incredibly generic note that appears to be intentionally vague so you can send it to a large batch of people at once. Even in the realm of online dating, people want to feel courted and feel as though the person contacting them is doing so because of a potential special connection. Most people do not want to get the impression that there is nothing particularly special about them, and a generic note that does not mention anything in particular will leave many people with the feeling that they have been spammed.

Your initial contact should reference something from that person's online profile. You can mention that you liked the way the person looked in a certain picture, or maybe that you have a hobby or passion in common. Try to prove to the person that you actually took the time to read through the profile.

Below are some examples of good first-time greetings, as well as some greetings that aren't quite as personal and thus won't result in a impressive first impression.

Bad: Hey, you're cute. Drop me a line and we'll chat.

Good: I love your smile. My guess is that you light up the stage when you do your acting at the community theater.

Bad: I don't know how you feel about religion, but if you're down with Eastern philosophy, then let me know.

Good: I see that you and I belong to the same denomination. I think we will have a lot to talk about!

Some people put quite a bit of effort into their online dating profiles, so when it becomes obvious that a person actually took the time to read the profile and to appreciate what they read, then it can be a great first impression. How would you feel if you labored over your online profile and then received a message from someone who obviously had not taken the time to read it at all? It does not make for a good first impression.

The Icky Factor

What is "the icky factor?" It is the feeling that you get when you meet someone and something is just not quite right. It doesn't necessarily mean that the person is a bad person or has something fundamentally wrong, but instead that the person just does not mesh well with you even though you can't really pinpoint what the issue is. Most people can decide rather quickly when they first meet someone else if there is an icky factor. Even if you can't tell exactly why you don't like a person, you are aware of the fact that you just don't like the person.

When you take the time to read through a profile thoroughly, then you may encounter an icky factor even if you have never laid eyes on the person outside the realm of online dating. You might not even be able to pinpoint exactly what it is you don't like about the person. Maybe the person's eyes seem a little too mischievous, or maybe something written within the person's profile just seems a little off. Whatever the reason, reading a person's profile all the way through just might let you know if there is an initial icky factor that makes you want to stay away from that person.

Trust your instincts. If you get the feeling that there is something not quite right about the person, or if you just get the sense that the two of you would not mesh well, then this can be a good sign that this isn't the person for you. Don't force yourself to respond to every single contact request your profile generates. Just because someone contacts you does not mean that you are obligated to respond, especially if that person's profile gives you a weird feeling.

Know Who You're Talking To

Never respond to an e-mail or some other form of contact without first reading the person's profile all the way through.

At first glance, some profiles may seem normal and attractive, but think about how many people may start out writing a profile and then, as they write, become more realistic as far as who they are or what they are looking for. For example, suppose a man writing a profile has just concluded a very messy and painful divorce. He may start writing his profile with every intention of appearing to be over his ex-wife and ready to meet someone new, but at some point in the text, hints may appear that suggest this man still has some issues to work out. Even if the beginning of a profile seems upbeat and inviting, read it all the way through to see if that theme is consistent or if something starts to falter partway through the profile.

Sometimes a profile will seem normal until the very end, when the writer decides that there is something important that must be revealed and will wait until the end of the profile to unveil it. For example, a profile for a woman might have an ending sentence along the lines of, "By the way, I don't intend on having children, and I'm not going to change my mind." Or perhaps a man's profile may end with, "If you have a problem with me spending every weekend out on the golf course, then you need to find someone else to date." Appreciate these small glimpses of candor because it is better to learn these things before ever contacting someone through an online dating site.

Online daters may also feel more comfortable making statements that they would never make in a public dating setting. Imagine a woman walking through a singles bar, loudly announcing that those who make less than $100,000 a year should not even bother to approach her because she doesn't want to meet anyone with a lower income level. This isn't something that you are likely to encounter in a public dating scene. But the format of online dating makes it completely possible (and acceptable) to make these demands and qualifications known so that anyone looking at a profile will be able to know right away if they "qualify" to initiate contact.

Other qualifying factors may be embedded within an online dating profile. People with preferences for certain ethnicities, religions, and educational levels often make these preferences clear within their profile, so you should review a profile before contacting someone or responding to an initial note.

Don't waste your time — or the time of the person you are thinking about contacting — by not bothering to read a profile in its entirety before making contact. You may be excited to start your online dating experience and may feel like a kid in a candy store, ready to sample everything offered. Using that same analogy, however, if you jump right in and sample everything without stopping to take the time to think about what you *really* want to sample, you will probably wind up with a stomach ache.

CASE STUDY: CAROL'S STORY

"'Who am I gonna meet? I'm 52 years old.'

I told myself it was dubious that I would meet someone at my age. After all, statistics seemed against me. Women in their 40s had improbable odds, so what would it be like after 50? Having recently separated from my husband, I gave myself six months to just relax and not even think about my next steps, but somewhere near the end of that sixth month,

I snapped a photo of myself from my cell phone while stuck in snarled Seattle commuter traffic, composed a profile, and posted myself on **www.JDate.com**. No expectations. If anything happened, it happened. If not, I was content on my own.

I had married late the first time at 38. I thought the odds would be in my favor. I was mature, had seen the world, built a career, and even had a child at 43. So, I thought it would last. It didn't. Remembering blind dates in my younger years, I dreaded meetings with guys who would only want to talk about themselves, guys who'd quibble over the check according to who ordered what, waiting for the telephone to ring, or worse, dreading having to tell them I wasn't interested. Casting fate to the wind, I let the chips fall where they may.

The first three men were unremarkable. I had two with a university professor who informed me that so many women were pursuing him, he felt it was his duty to meet them all. That simply left him no more time for me. The next complained about his ex-wife throughout dinner, and the third was incredibly scruffy and then told me he didn't like women who cursed. Whoops! I blew that one in the first sentence.

I was resolute that I'd let men pursue me; I was not going to initiate anything. When I noticed a guy online in a black turtleneck, I was delighted when he contacted me. He started off with the usual banter, but there was something different about him. He loved Asia. So did I. He lived there for a while, and so had I.

CASE STUDY: CAROL'S STORY

He came from the New York City metropolitan area. Me too. We were both separated recently and just taking first steps in online dating. He had a wry kind of wit and yet was rather sweet. We e-mailed for about a month before we met and, during those weeks, I became increasingly intrigued.

But then again, he wrote that skiing was his passion, he loved snowstorms, and that he was looking for someone to share the thrill of downhill powder skiing with. I answered his e-mail with 'I must be honest. I hate the winter, am deathly afraid of heights, and haven't been skiing since I was about ten. If that's important to you, I'm not your soul mate, but might end up being a good friend.'

He never responded to that e-mail. We wrote tentative, brief notes, and then they grew longer. We arranged to meet at Magic Mouse Toys in Seattle on our first date, on Christmas Eve. I was nervous, surprisingly. I stopped off to see my divorce attorney after work, dropped in at Sephora™ and made myself up, dousing just a little too much perfume behind my ears, and then took a deep breath and sauntered into Magic Mouse as relaxed as I could appear. Bruce appeared about 20 minutes late, flashing a sweet smile and giving me a quick hug. I felt his eyes looking me over. I blushed.

He asked me what my son, Remy, liked in the store. Oh my God, he was 8, so he liked just about everything, but I pointed to a couple of things as we browsed. Bruce excused himself for a few minutes (I suspected he was using the restroom). When he returned, he suggested we go for drinks. When we got to the café, he nonchalantly pulled out three of the items I had described as Remy's favorites. 'Tell him they're from you,' he said as he handed them to me. I took a step back, stared hard at him, and said, 'Where have you been all my life?'

We ordered champagne, talked for hours, and, well…the rest is history. We'll be celebrating the fourth anniversary of that evening this Christmas Eve, and our third wedding anniversary in June."

CHAPTER 8

Getting Your Feet Wet

If you have made it this far and have yet to take the leap into online dating, congratulations. You are well-prepared with regards to how the different popular dating sites work, and you know how to craft a profile that will grab the attention of the type of people you would like to meet. You know to trust your instincts when it comes to the other singles in the databases, and you know that in most cases, it is better to take your time and do your research instead of trusting that everyone is who they say they are.

Now, it's time to get started.

It's completely normal to feel a little apprehensive about online dating, especially if you haven't dated in a long time. For some people, such as those who are newly divorced, widowed, or who have simply been single for a while, online dating can be a safe way to re-enter the dating world. Nonetheless, it can also be a relatively scary experience because, for some people, the idea of placing an online profile on a dating site puts them in a vulnerable position. Know that these feelings of vulnerability are normal and are the same emotions you would probably feel walking into a singles function. You can also take solace in the fact that you are probably going to meet some very interesting people, and may even stumble upon the love of your life online.

Getting your feet wet with online dating can be exciting! Embrace the potential of the process and try to have fun with it. Don't build your expectations up too high in the beginning, and allow yourself plenty of time to ease into the process. Online dating communities are bona fide subcultures, so like with any other community, you'll need a little time to learn all the rules and assimilate. If you are like most people, however, it won't take long before you are deeply enmeshed into the online dating community and having a great time.

If you want to increase your chances of enjoying your online dating experience while also increasing your chances of meeting other people you are compatible with, follow the three rules for online dating.

Rule One: Always Be Honest

Don't create an online dating profile that is merely a representation of who you *want* to be. Being deceitful will only delay or prevent you from meeting someone special. A common problem is the belief that you are inherently flawed. Though it is certainly true that no one is perfect, it is also important to recognize that even your flaws make you who you are. You are unique and have attributes that other people can find attractive, even if you don't find these attributes attractive yourself.

When you are asked questions by other online daters, answer the questions honestly. Don't think to yourself, "How can I stretch the truth in my response to make me more attractive and appealing to this person?" Answer truthfully. Yes, you want to make yourself look good, but not to the point of deceit.

You will be faced with questions on the initial questionnaire and from other members that may tempt you to want to fudge on the truth. One common example of this is when it comes to body type. Almost all of the online dating sites will ask you to specify what your body type is, be it athletic, thin, a few extra pounds, or overweight. You may think that your profile picture should be enough to reveal your body type to potential dates, but photos can be deceiving. After all, it is unlikely that you will post a profile picture that is unflattering, so you can't make the assumption that your photo will tell people everything they need to know about your body. Don't lie about your body when you are filling out your questionnaire or when responding to another member of the dating site. Remember that there is someone out there who finds your body type appealing, regardless of what your body type is.

People will feel betrayed if they discover something different than what you tell them or what is listed on your profile. Keep this in mind: You have little chance of having someone fall in love with you online based on lies and later stay in love with you because your true personality shines through. No one wants to be lied to. Present a realistic portrayal of who you are so you can find someone who is interested in you, instead of the false character you have created.

Answering Questions

You're going to be asked a lot of questions by the people who contact you, and by the people you initiate contact with. Answer these questions as honestly as possible, while still portraying yourself in an attractive light. For example, a common question you will probably encounter is, "What happened in your last relationship?" If your last relationship ended messily because your mate cheated on and humiliated you, you don't need to reveal every last detail of what happened. While you want to tell the truth ("My last relationship ended abruptly, and it wasn't easy for me"), you don't want to use the person as a free therapist ("Do you think there is something wrong with me that makes people want to cheat on me?") or as a sounding board for how upset you are over the situation ("I really think that all men are scum, but I sure hope you can prove me wrong.").

Phrase your answers in a positive light, but do not deceive other people. If you aren't legally divorced, don't say that you are. Instead, explain the situation in a simple and positive way. You may be surprised to find that there are people online who not only understand your situation, but who don't necessarily see it as a negative thing. After all, you aren't the first person within the online dating community to have a few extra pounds, to be in the middle of a custody battle with an ex, or to not be wealthy.

While you want to make sure that you aren't lying to anyone, you also do not want to use the opportunity to answer questions as a way to reveal your entire life story to someone else. For instance, if someone contacts you and asks what you do for a living, this is not the time to send the person a veritable résumé that highlights your professional achievements since you graduated from college. Instead, simply answer the question with a positive response like, "I work for a financial services company as an advisor, and I really love what I do," or "I work at a preschool as a teacher's aide, and it's a great fit for me because I enjoy playing with kids all day long." You may be tempted to respond to questions with an aggressive diatribe about how angry you are about your past relationships, but the first e-mail correspondence with a potential date is certainly not the time to launch into a complete relationship history that is filled with the mistakes you made and your hurt emotions.

Responding to Sensitive Questions

You may receive some questions from potential dates you don't want to answer — or, you might just not know how to answer.

If you receive a question that sends up a red flag that indicates to that the other person is definitely not right for you, then you can chalk it up as a fortunate discovery early on, or you can instead pursue the matter to find out if there is a reason why the question was asked.

Remember that sometimes things don't come out the way they were intended when they are typed instead of spoken. Something that completely offends you in an e-mail from a potential date may be nothing more than a misunderstanding, or could even be a typo. Can you imagine if the person was trying to ask you if you like the Red Sox, but instead typed Red Sex by mistake and didn't catch the error? You might assume that "red sex" is something horribly devious or some covert term that you aren't familiar with.

Before you rattle off a disgusted response about how the person should never contact you again, or before you delete the person's correspondence entirely, take a look at the body of the message in full. Does everything else seem to be quite normal and pleasant? If the odd remark seems really out of place, then there is a good chance that it wasn't meant as you perceived it. If you just can't make sense of it, but you like everything else about the person so far, then there is nothing wrong with responding and asking for clarification.

However, sometimes sensitive questions are asked and are fully intended as they are written. The fact is that some people simply feel more comfortable with asking inappropriate questions either because that is just how their personality is, or maybe they have been dating online for so long that they have been desensitized to the initial courting stage of correspondence with someone new. Some people just seem to become comfortable quickly when it comes to asking sensitive or inappropriate questions.

Whether you respond to these questions is up to you, but always remember to protect your security, as well as to think long-term about how the person will perceive you. For example, if someone contacts you with a sexually explicit message and tells you that the two of you need to meet up as soon as possible, it certainly isn't a very good idea to respond with an equally explicit message along with your home address. If a quick sexual encounter is what you are looking for from online dating, then these are the types of messages you can expect; however, that does not mean you should throw caution to the wind.

Once in a while, you may encounter questions that may not be uncomfortable to most people, but because of your life's circumstances, you have a hard time answering the questions. Suppose your parents were killed in a horrific car accident when you were young; you probably won't respond well to a question regarding your parents. Or suppose you are a recovering alcoholic; you probably won't respond well to a question asking about your favorite type of wine. When you encounter questions like this, keep in mind that the person asking the question has no familiarity with your life story other than what you placed on your profile. For this reason, you cannot expect to gloss over a simple question and ignore it — or worse yet, get upset about the question — and have the other person view this as a reasonable response. If you don't want to explain why you don't feel comfortable answering a question, at least have the courtesy to acknowledge the question and assure the person that you will be happy to discuss it after the two of you get to know each other a little better. For example, the question about your parents could easily be answered with "My parents are both deceased." You don't need to go into

> Oh what a tangled web we weave,
> when first we practice to deceive.
>
> -Sir Walter Scott

all the details. The question about your favorite wine could be responded to with a simple, "I don't drink wine" or even "I used to love a good Chablis, but I don't drink wine anymore." Answer the question depending on your comfort level, but never reply with a lie.

Rule Two: Take Your Time and Don't Rush

If you haven't gotten started with online dating yet, get ready to get enmeshed into it pretty quickly. Most people find that once they start the process of online dating, they get a lot more involved with it than they initially thought. Some people find that they spend a great deal of time sifting through the databases of singles and dedicate quite a bit of time to corresponding with others. In other words, if you thought that getting involved with online dating was going to be a passive activity, then chances are, you will quickly find that you were wrong.

This is not to say that everyone dedicates hours of time to the online dating experience. There are indeed some people who simply place a profile on a site and only respond to a few of the messages they receive. Most people, however, enjoy the process of looking through the profiles of other singles and may find themselves staying up past their usual bedtimes in an attempt to view all the compatible singles online.

Pace yourself. While you may have the urge to contact every single attractive person you encounter online and respond to every correspondence you receive, you should slow down and take an objective look at things. You don't want to wind up in a situation where you send out so many notes to so many people that you start to mix everyone up. That's not looking for love; that's collecting friends. If you just want to meet friends and build your social network, join a social networking Web site instead of an online dating site. If, on the other hand, you want to meet someone special, then approach the task with some patience and dedication.

Use the analogy of walking through a room full of single people. Do you stop to speak to every single person? Do you take the time to get to know everyone who shows an interest in you? In any situation where you are meeting new people, whether it is online or in a face-to-face setting, it is a good idea to be a little picky. This does not mean that you should be hypercritical of people or that you should surround yourself with an air of conceit, but instead realize that if someone is not compatible with you, then you don't need to force it to happen. Remember: When it comes to online dating, there are *always* more fish in the sea. Slow down and enjoy the process. You will have a much better time with online dating if you don't turn it into a rapid conquest.

Contacting Other People

Unless your plan is to create a profile and then make other people contact you, you will probably spend time initiating contact with other people. This is another instance in which it pays to pace yourself and not get carried away with contacting too many people at once. Think about the bigger picture when it comes to contacting potential dates online and, if necessary, refer to the analogy of walking into a room full of single people. What are the odds that everyone in the room is going to be compatible with you? Just like that room full of single people, chances are that, although there may be plenty of attractive people in the single's database, only a small percentage of these people may actually meet your stricter relationship criteria.

If you find yourself compelled to contact too many people and feel as though you must rush through the process, place a note on your computer or somewhere on your desk that reminds you to slow down. Even if it's a sticky note that simply says, "Slow Down!" or "Good things come to those who wait," this can serve as a visual reminder that though online dating is a lot of fun and can expose you to a wide variety of people, it isn't a race. Unless your goal is to rack up as many contacts as possible, the best thing to do is to take your time.

If you know what you are looking for — and stick to the criteria you set — you will spend a lot less time sending out communications to people who ultimately will not be compatible with you. If you find yourself mumbling, "Oh, hey, there's a cute one!" and quickly sending out a note, then you're not being as selective as you should be. Look beyond the picture and take the time to read through a person's profile before you ever initiate communication.

Online dating comes with plenty of shortcuts if you want to meet a great deal of people within in a short period of time. Most of the larger sites offer a feature that allows you to "wink," "flirt," or "poke" someone, which is supposed to be a quick way to say "Hello, I like the look of your profile. Take a look at mine and let me know what you think." The danger of sending these mini-introductions to people without first taking the time to read through the profile is that you may get sidetracked dating someone you aren't compatible with — which you would have learned if you had bothered to read through the person's profile and took your time with the process.

Meeting People

If you have chemistry with someone you found on an online dating site, you may find that you develop a sense of urgency to meet that person, especially if you have talked on the phone or e-mailed and have built a nice rapport. Again, this is an instance where you should exercise caution and not rush into it. After you have spent more time sifting through online dating sites, you will soon discover that there are some people who go through new profiles, contact people, and aggressively pursue them because they know that the person is new to the system and has not yet learned to be very selective. Save yourself the trouble by not rushing to meet someone.

There is no magical timeline that you should follow when you're ready to meet someone. Generally, it is not a good idea to meet someone online and meet them in person on the same day. You will typically need a little time to simmer over the person's profile and the things the person says. Some people who date online have a fear that all the good singles are going to get snatched up quickly, so if they don't act quickly, they will miss out on the love of their life. But online dating is *not* a clearance sale. You don't have to be the first one in, and you don't have to elbow other people to get to the best deals. It doesn't work like that.

You also don't want to take too long to meet someone because it might start to make the other person nervous. You don't want a potential date wondering why you are stalling on having an initial face-to-face meeting. Don't stall, but don't rush. There is a fine balance between the two, but after you have become acquainted with online dating, you will start to understand the balance you need to achieve. You'll also find that it is different for every match. You may have the urge to meet someone who you really hit it off with, while another person might elicit in you only minor anticipation for a first meeting. Trust your instincts, but don't allow yourself to get carried away.

You will know when you are ready to meet someone. You should take as much time as you need to acquaint yourself with someone and get comfortable via messages and phone conversations before setting up a face-to-face meeting. Realize that some people who have been on the Internet dating scene for a while may need less time to get comfortable and might be a little more ready to jump right into personally meeting someone, especially if all previous meetings have been positive experiences.

Don't allow someone else to talk you into meeting before you're ready. There is no magic timeline that reveals exactly when you should meet someone face-to-face, although you may quickly find a pattern arising that dictates when you start to feel comfortable enough to meet someone from an online dating site. It is at this point that you can make the rules for yourself, such as "I need to chat with someone for two weeks before we can meet in person" or "I need at least ten phone conversations before I will meet face-to-face." You may feel more comfortable with some people than others with regards to meeting up in a public place, so listen to what your gut instincts tell you and follow accordingly.

Rule Three: Don't Take Everything to Heart

If you haven't yet posted a profile, then you're at a great advantage to learn this now before you must learn it the hard way: Online dating will have its low points. You simply can't expect everyone you contact to want to contact you, and you may even experience very unpleasant comments from a few people. This should not deter you from becoming involved with online dating. The fact of the matter is that any time you put yourself out there and allow yourself to be vulnerable, there are inevitably going to be people who capitalize on that because of their own self-esteem issues. Whether it's your friends and family taunting you because you created a profile on a dating Web site, or another online dater sending you an insulting note, as long as you are confident in yourself, this will not be something that changes your desire to meet someone special online.

The trick is to find the delicate balance between investing yourself into online dating without putting too much of your heart into it. It's almost an impossible balance to achieve perfectly, but it is an important one. You don't want to be callous and flippant when it comes to online dating (unless that is how you really are) because you will likely have a hard time meeting someone that way, but on the other side of the coin, you don't want to put your entire heart and soul into online dating because there is always a chance that you can get your heart broken.

Remember that online dating is really nothing more than an introductory service; the database introduces you to a variety of singles and gives you a means to contact them. Whether or not the people like you, want to date you, or eventually fall in love with you is up to you and the other person. Don't expect that joining an online dating site will guarantee that you find love. You should only expect that it will expose you to a wide variety of people who may be compatible with what you're looking for in a potential mate.

Responses

Suppose you find a profile that you immediately become enamored with. The person is not only attractive, but also accomplished and clever. You love everything about the person's profile, and you are completely confident that the two of you would hit it off splendidly. You send a note to the person and anxiously await a reply because he or she may very well prove to be the love of your life, as far as you are concerned. Unfortunately, the person does not fall as equally in love with your profile and sends you a nice note to say "Thanks, but no thanks." Or maybe you never hear back from the person at all.

Rejection hurts, no matter what form it comes in. You may be surprised at the level of pain you can feel from being rejected by someone while dating online, especially considering you have never even met the person face-to-face. It's completely normal to feel angry, sad, or confused when rejected by someone else online, so allow yourself those emotions. But move on and continue with your search.

You have to decide whether or not you will respond to every communication you receive from your profile or not, but you have no control over whether people respond to you or not. There is no way to guarantee that you will always get a note back from the people you send notes to, and in some instances, you will never hear from some of the people whom you attempt to contact. Don't set your expectations too high. You simply cannot expect that everyone you contact will respond.

If you find that the *majority* of people who you contact do not respond to you, then you need to ask yourself some questions, such as "Is there something I need to change on my profile?" or "Do I need to change the wording in the initial contact I send to potential dates?" If, on the other hand, there is no trend that suggests that most people do not respond to you, then just accept it and move on. For all you know, the other person may have met someone else already, has computer issues, or simply is not attracted to you. Don't overanalyze the situation because it won't accomplish anything.

Compatibility

Here is something you may not be expecting, and you may be quite taken aback to realize: There is a chance that you can go through an entire compatibility screening on a dating Web site only to discover that there are *no compatible matches for you* based on the system used by the site and the responses you gave on the compatibility questionnaire.

This can be quite disheartening. After all, if you just spent an hour filling out a lengthy questionnaire in anticipation of being matched with someone who is perfect for you, receiving no compatible matches can seem like a slap in the face. Sites that offer compatibility matching usually offer up alternate matches based on a loose match in this instance, but it's still a situation that may make you pause and get a little mad at the process. You might wonder if there is something wrong with the Web site — or perhaps even if there is something wrong with you.

Relax. There is nothing wrong with you. Just because a preliminary review does not produce a perfectly compatible match certainly does not mean that there is no match for you at all. Your match may just be on a different site, or maybe the Web site just does not use reliable compatibility methods.

You may want to think about how you answered some of the

questions to figure out why you don't have any compatible matches.

Did you restrict the geographic area where your match can live? Did you say that money means a great deal to you? Did you say that you are often sad or that you have problems with impulsivity? Did you say that certain things were absolutely essential, such as a person being a non-smoker or having a certain religious preference? When you respond to questions with absolutes, you are less likely to have a wide variety of potential matches. Also, when you wholeheartedly admit to undesirable traits, you also restrict the number of people you can be deemed compatible with. You already know that you shouldn't lie about what type of person you are, but you also don't need to cast a negative light on yourself.

On the other hand, you certainly do not want to compromise who you really are and what you truly want to find in another person. It's fine to re-evaluate your needs and to reconsider the demands you make as long as these changes don't force you to go outside your comfort zone. For example, if you know that without a doubt you want to date someone who does not drink alcohol at all, know that although this limits the number of suitable singles you will find online, it also provides an absolute qualifying factor.

If you find yourself frustrated by the lack of suitable singles that you find online because of whatever qualifying factors you set, keep in mind that there are plenty of dating Web sites online that are specific to certain lifestyles and beliefs. Don't sacrifice your core beliefs and the things that are important to you in an attempt to broaden your selection of compatible singles. You might be able to find more people online who are acceptable under your new standards, but when it comes down to it, are you going to be happy sacrificing what you are really looking for in a match? Don't cheat yourself out of the things that can really make you content just because you want more singles to choose from.

If the site gives you the option to redo the questionnaire, then you can consider doing so, but you don't want to change your responses to untruths. Instead, be willing to take a look at the profiles that the site deems as having loose compatibility with you to see if you are interested. If the site allows you to freely peruse the database of singles, go ahead and do so. Don't take it as an insult or indication of there being something wrong with you if the site can't immediately match you with someone else with a high degree of compatibility. It doesn't mean that there is anything wrong with you or that you will never find the love of your life. It just means that at that particular point in time, there is no one registered on the dating site who appears fully compatible with you, based on the answers you gave in the initial questionnaire.

Rejected

Some dating Web sites go beyond claiming to not have any suitable matches for a person; instead, the Web site flatly rejects the person after the initial questionnaire is completed. If you are rejected by a dating Web site, then your only options are to either choose a different site to use or to redo the initial questionnaire and change some of your answers. This can be frustrating for a couple of different reasons. First, some dating sites that reject potential members — such as eHarmony — may not reveal why you received a rejection. Instead, you will simply be informed that you can't be matched. For this reason, you may not ever know why you were rejected by the site, and this can be frustrating. Secondly, if you took the time to answer every question as accurately as possible and really felt as though the answers were an accurate representation of you, there is a good chance that a rejection will be a little disheartening. Always remember that the system isn't rejecting *you*, but instead is just rejecting the way you answered a series of questions. Try not to take offense to the rejection.

Although there is not a definitive listing of reasons for rejections on eHarmony or other sites that reject certain applicants, there are a few instances that may increase your chances of getting rejected, depending on the site:

♥ You are married or separated, but not yet legally divorced.

♥ You are under the minimum age limit of the Web site.

♥ The responses to your questions reveal a trend of emotional instability.

♥ The responses to your questions are so erratic that it appears as though you randomly selected answers without truly considering your selections.

Dating sites that cater to certain religious denominations may reject people who do not fall into the same denominational category, just like some sites specific to wealthy people may reject singles who do not meet the minimum net worth (or income) requirements for membership.

A rejection from a dating Web site does not indicate that there is no match out there for you at all, but instead is simply an indication that you should try a different site. Also keep in mind that if you are still married, this will disqualify you from some of the mainstream dating sites. Additionally, there are many sites that aren't set up to match people of the same sex. Don't get discouraged if you're unable to use a particular site. Do you really want to give your money to a site that does not want to match you? Instead of lamenting about the rejection, chalk it up to experience and find another dating site.

Think of it as though the dating site that rejected you is doing you a favor. If you're looking for someone similar to you,

you're certainly not going to find anyone suitable on a site that rejects people like you, right?

CASE STUDY: JENNIFER'S STORY

"Before I was married, I met a lot of guys online. They obviously didn't turn out to be The One. Most of the guys I talked to online were just looking for sex or to get a relationship outside their current relationship. I met a couple of married men. No one really wanted a commitment. In my experience, the only guys who are looking for a relationship are the nerds that are either old or are just nerdy.

I did meet a guy online that I moved out to Orange County for. I think he was just an excuse for me to get out of my hometown because a couple months after I moved out here, we broke up. I didn't see myself marrying him. Through dating men from the Internet, I found out who I was and what I did or didn't want in my future husband. It also taught me a lot about men, like what to look for when he isn't interested. You know that book, *He's Just Not That Into You*? Yeah, I could have helped write it. But I wouldn't be the person I am today if it wasn't for that whole experience.

Before he met me, my husband met a girl online that he moved to Illinois for, but it didn't work out and he broke up with her. She was his first girlfriend so he didn't know any better. I was with two men that I can remember who were married that I had met online. One I knew was married, but I think I just wanted to get physical. I met him at his house and it was a bad situation. His little boy was there. He was a detective, too. Then, we met one more time after that when he was on duty. The other guy didn't tell me until after we met in person and he was separated, but I continued to date him until he told me that they were thinking of reconciling so I left and didn't talk to him again. I was done with that.

I think about it now and wonder, 'What was I thinking?' I know that I think of the experiences from time to time and I don't know if I wish I could do it all over again and do it differently or not. I thought I was looking for Mr. Right, but I knew deep down I wouldn't find him online…and I didn't."

Overcoming Fear

Does the fear of rejection stop you from contacting the people you are really attracted to, or does it stop you from even putting a profile up on a dating site? The fear of rejection is completely normal. No one wants to go into a situation knowing that they will be rejected, and many people opt to instead avoid any situation that may result in a rejection. Online dating does indeed open you up to the potential of getting rejected, but this fear of rejection should not paralyze your efforts of meeting your match online.

How do you get rid of this fear of rejection? Although there is no foolproof way, one method often used by actors (a group of people who may arguably be the most likely to get rejected professionally, but must still keep going if they want to keep working) is to try to change the way they look at rejection. Acting coaches often urge their students to start looking at rejection in a different way. What if you actually sought out rejection? What if you forced yourself to do something every single day that may open you up to getting rejected? What if getting rejected was actually a *success?*

While it is true that you don't want to get rejected by the people who you find appealing online, it is also true that if you can stop fearing rejection, then you can open up a new world of possibilities. Instead of clicking past the profile of someone who is incredibly attractive, you would drop the person a note with enthusiasm. Instead of avoiding accomplished singles because you do not want to feel inferior, you would initiate communications with these people despite their impressive lives. When you change your frame of mind to actually seek rejection, then something interesting happens. You no longer face anxiety when you enter into a situation where rejection is possible, but instead, you look forward to the outcome because you're actually expecting rejection.

Make no mistake about it: This does *not* mean that you should aspire to find specific people online who will reject you based on things you know they aren't looking for. If you're rail-thin, don't contact someone who specified within the profile that the only type of person he or she is looking for must be big and beautiful. Instead, it means that you should not stop yourself from contacting people based on a fear of rejection or a fear of the unknown. If someone appears to be fully compatible with you, but seems somehow unattainable based on the person's attractiveness, success, or some other trait that intimidates you, your blatant disregard for rejection will prompt you to go ahead and contact the person instead of skipping past the profile because you automatically assume that you might get rejected.

It isn't an easy process. Actors take a long time to embrace this idea, and some of them never do, so there is no reason why you should expect to have a sudden epiphany that allows you to go for what you want without a fear of rejection. If you can change your outlook just a little, though, you may find that you open your life up to a whole new set of possibilities.

When You Are the One Doing the Rejecting

It is inevitable that you are not going to like everyone who contacts you through your profile. There will be people who just don't fit what you are looking for in a potential mate, and there will be people who repulse you. Either way, you need to decide how to handle the task of rejecting the people who initiate contact with you who don't appeal to you in the least for whatever reason.

Follow the same basic rules that you would want someone else to follow when rejecting you: Be nice, be prompt, and don't lead someone on.

You need to make the decision of whether you want to respond to everyone who contacts you. Some people would argue that it is simply common courtesy to respond to people even if you aren't interested in them whatsoever because the least you can do is to thank them for their interest and let them know that you aren't interested. On the other hand, other people would argue that not replying to these people is preferred because that way you aren't really rejecting them, but instead you are just fading from their memory. Which do you choose? Do you send a nice note to the people who you don't want to meet to wish them well, or do you instead delete the note and don't even bother to acknowledge it?

The answer depends on your personal preference. How do *you* want people to react to your initial contact when they aren't interested in you? Would you prefer that they send back a friendly note that says "Thanks, but I'm not interested," or would you rather not face that rejection and never hear from them again? It's a good rule of thumb to react to this situation in the way you would want other people to react to you. By reacting in this way, you at least know that you are treating people the way you want to be treated, and sometimes, this can make the act of rejecting someone just a little bit easier.

Rejecting people can be difficult, especially when your goal is to make yourself as attractive as possible to other people. You want to be seen in the best light — even by the people who you don't want to date — so this makes it tough to face the task of telling someone that you are rejecting them. How should you go about it? If you make the decision to reply to people you don't want to date, to simply thank them for their note and to wish them well, you need to figure out the best way to do it.

Consider writing a form letter that you can use for each rejection. It shouldn't be horribly generic, but you don't need to make it personalized for each person. You don't necessarily have to pinpoint the reason why you don't want to meet the person either. If you decide to reply to everyone, keep it pleasant, but don't make it too friendly; otherwise, the same people might reply to you again in the hopes that your friendly note was a covert attempt to play coy.

You also don't have to send an elaborate note that apologizes for not being attracted to the person. Don't explain why the two of you would never click. Simply state the facts: You appreciate being contacted, but it's not a match.

Here is an example of a form note that you can keep on hand to send to people who contact you, but you don't want to further contact:

Dear _____

Thanks for the note. Even though I'm not the right person for you, I have no doubt you'll meet someone special. I wish you luck.

Regards,

_____

Remember, you don't have to contact people who contact you unless you want to pursue the possibility of getting to know them. Replying to a note opens up the lines of communications, good or bad, so after a while you may decide that you prefer to just delete the notes you get from people who you aren't interested in. Then again, you never know when you might become great friends with someone who you don't want to date, so there is indeed some merit in replying to everyone. Ultimately, it is your decision, so act based on your preferences.

No matter which method you choose, do not use this as a way to ridicule people. Suppose you receive a note from someone you have never met who sends you a long, heartfelt note that talks about how someday the two of you may wind up dancing together in a field of daisies, or something equally sentimental. Before you reply with ridicule and criticize the sender for getting entirely too emotional over a stranger, realize that probably one of two things has happened: Either the sender sends this note to *everyone* as a form letter and is trying to appeal to people as a sentimental romantic, or the sender really thought there was a potential for a connection and spent a lot of time forming what he or she thought was the perfect introduction to open the lines of communication. Don't insult the person or set out to prove what a sappy, ridiculous note it was. Instead, either send a form letter or just delete the note.

You may get more than one attempt of communication from the same person. People who have been dating online for some time realize that notes are quickly skimmed and deleted a lot of the time, so a second appeal for a meeting isn't uncommon. Some people just like the thrill of the chase and will be relentless. If you receive multiple notes from the same person, then decide if you want to just keep deleting the messages or instead send a note of thanks, but no thanks. Then again, maybe you want to be chased and this is exactly the type of thing you find attractive; if this is the case, then maybe it's meant to be.

Initiating Contact

What is the best way to initiate contact with other online daters you are interested in? One rule to follow is this: There is not one single best way to approach everyone. You will soon find a preferred method of contacting people, but you need to be flexible and get a feel for how people actually want to be contacted. For example, some people may specify in their profiles that they do not want to receive random "flirts" or "pokes" and would much rather receive an actual note from potential matches. If you ignore this stated preference because you always start your communications the easy way (with a "flirt" or "poke"), then you have already disregarded the person's preference and will inadvertently start off the communication on a sour note.

Depending on how many people you anticipate contacting to initiate communication, you can compose a form letter that you can use for everyone with portions of it personalized for each person. On the other hand, if it is your intention to be incredibly selective and only contact people who really catch your eye, a form letter will prove ineffective because chances are, you will want to thoroughly personalize your communications for each person.

Whatever method you decide to use, remember the advice from Lori Gorshow in Chapter 5 that says you should always demonstrate that you actually took the time to read the person's profile. You should specify what it was about the profile that caught your attention. Too many people who date online simply blanket the database with a bunch of notes to people, so the recipients of these notes grow tired of getting generic notes that don't prove a real interest at all. The notes usually wind up being deleted and never get responded to. Don't let your attempts at communication seem generic and part of a mass mailing.

Think about mail you receive in your postal mail box. A written letter from someone will certainly take precedence over advertisements that go to everyone in the neighborhood. You are probably excited to receive the personalized note, but even though the ads can be somewhat useful, you don't get quite as excited about them because you know everyone else received the exact same mail. Don't let your messages to other online daters fall into the category of mass mailings. Strive to send an initial communication that seems more like a personalized letter.

If you do want to use a form letter, consider something along these lines, filling in the blanks with personalized information that not only proves you really read the profile, but that also makes the person feel special:

Hi _____,

When I found your profile, I was immediately intrigued. I am so impressed with _____! You and I share the common trait of _____. I would love to talk to you and get to know you better. Have a look at my profile and drop me a line so we can chat.

You don't have to give your real name in the first communication if you aren't comfortable using it. This is completely acceptable in the realm of online dating. Consider waiting to reveal your real name until after the person you've contacted replies to you and shows some interest. There are a couple of reasons for this. Primarily, it is a security issue, and secondarily, it also protects you in a psychological way. If you never share your actual name with people who wind up rejecting you, it may be easier for you to deal with because, in a way, they aren't rejecting the real you. For some people, this helps them distance themselves from the feelings of rejection.

Some dating sites make it a little harder to initiate contact with other singles, but this is usually done by the request of the member. For example, some users will set their privacy settings to where people must answer a series of questions before you can send a note. This is a safeguard set by the users to make sure that the people contacting them aren't sending out initial contact requests with reckless abandon and also to screen out some people who may not be compatible. Some Web sites allow users to choose their own qualifying questions, while others will allow users to choose from a list of questions that are prewritten.

Should you have other singles answer a few questions before they are allowed to contact you? Not all dating sites offer this feature, but if the site you use does offer this option, then you will have to decide whether or not to utilize it. Some people may find a series of questions intimidating, but as long as the questions you choose aren't too daunting, there is no reason why you shouldn't require a few answers. Choose some fun questions that also pertain to what you are looking for in a match.

Beyond Messages

Depending on which online dating site you decide to use, you may have more options for initiating contact with appealing singles beyond sending an e-mail message through the site's server. Keep in mind that some of the features that allow you to contact other site users may cost extra or may not be included in a regular membership. Even though they cost extra, though, they may be preferable to simply sending a message through the server.

Some dating sites offer live chat options that can be a lot of fun. With this feature, you can either hop into a chat room and talk with a variety of people, or you can attempt to initiate a private chat with a specific person. In fact, some dating Web sites will feature links to online chat with people directly from their profiles. If you are looking at a person's profile and are intrigued, you can check to see if that person is online, and if so, you can request a live chat.

There are advantages and disadvantages to using a live chat option. A definite advantage is the immediate contact. There is no waiting for the other person to decide whether to reply to your message, but instead you get instant access to the person.

This isn't always a positive thing, though. If a person accepts your chat request but doesn't have the opportunity to take a look at your profile, then it can be an awkward conversation. This person doesn't know anything about you and may feel a little blindsided by the request. Instant message chatting can also bring with it the problems associated with having a conversation electronically. If you aren't well-versed in the lingo associated with instant messaging, then a conversation like this can be confusing and a little frustrating. You also run into the problem of not being able to hear the fluctuations in a person's voice or view their body language, and this can translate into some confusion if any statements are vague or confusing.

If you are unfamiliar with the acronyms and emoticons that are used for instant messaging, keep in mind that while some of them can be figured out if you take a second to think about it, others can be downright confusing. If all else fails, ask for clarification or quickly hop onto a search to look up what the acronym means. To get you started, here is a brief list of some of the terms and symbols that you may encounter if you use an instant messaging feature on a dating site:

- ♥ ?4U – Question for you
- ♥ ASAP – As soon as possible
- ♥ ASL – Age/sex/location
- ♥ ATM – At the moment
- ♥ AYR – Awaiting your reply
- ♥ B4 – Before

- ♥ BBL – Be back later
- ♥ BF – Boyfriend
- ♥ BFF – Best friends forever
- ♥ BRB – Be right back
- ♥ BTW – By the way
- ♥ CTN – Can't talk now
- ♥ CU – See you
- ♥ CUL8R – See you later
- ♥ CYA – See ya
- ♥ CYE – Check your e-mail
- ♥ DL – Download
- ♥ F2F – Face to face
- ♥ GF – Girlfriend
- ♥ GL – Good luck
- ♥ GR8 – Great
- ♥ GTG – Got to go
- ♥ IMO – In my opinion
- ♥ IDK – I don't know
- ♥ IRL – In real life
- ♥ J/K – Just kidding
- ♥ KIT – Keep in touch
- ♥ L8R – Later
- ♥ LOL – Laughing out loud
- ♥ LTR – Long-term relationship
- ♥ MMB – Message me back
- ♥ OIC – Oh I see
- ♥ PDA – Public display of affection
- ♥ PITA – Pain in the ass
- ♥ Pls – Please
- ♥ Ppl – People
- ♥ ROFL – Rolling on the floor laughing
- ♥ RUOK – Are you okay
- ♥ SN – Screen name
- ♥ Str8 – Straight
- ♥ TBDL – To be discussed later
- ♥ TMI – Too much information
- ♥ TTYL – Talk to you later
- ♥ Thx – Thanks
- ♥ UR – You are
- ♥ WBS – Write back soon
- ♥ W/E – Whatever

:) – Happy

:(– Sad

:-) – Happy with a nose

:-(– Sad with a nose

I –O – Yawn

:-D – Laughter

>:) – Evil grin

%-(– Confused

B-) – Batman/Glasses

:-I – Indifferent

:-0 – Yelling/Surprised

;-) – Winking

:* – Drunk / Kiss

8) – Cool

8:P – Sticking tongue out/ silly

:-& – Tongue-tied

0:-) – Angel

Most of the sites offering online chat will provide a pull-down menu that will allow you to pick among a variety of emoticons (also known as "smileys") so you won't have to fumble with the keys trying to figure out how to make a devilish grin or a winking face. Try not to rely on these emoticons or acronyms too much when chatting with someone else via instant messenger. Although these tools do make it easier to get your message across quickly, they can depersonalize the experience and make it feel much less intimate. It is much more difficult to get to know someone when the bulk of the conversation is nothing more than acronyms and smileys.

You can avoid all of these abbreviations — yet still enjoy instant chatting — if the dating site you use offers Webcam conversations. This allows you to talk to other singles using your computer while also utilizing your Webcam so you can have a face-to-face encounter from your computer. This isn't something you should jump right into; after all, keep in mind that the other person will actually get to see you through your Webcam, so this is not something you want to agree to if you're sitting at home in sweats and a stained T-shirt. If you know that you are planning on participating in a Webcam through a dating site, dress appropriately, make yourself appealing, and make sure that the area surrounding you within your home is not messy. A Webcam is like a first date without either one of you ever having to leave your home, so prepare just as you would for a date outside the home.

Something you should keep in mind with regards to online Webcams is that some people use this feature on dating sites for the sole purpose of having sexually provocative conversations, so don't be surprised if the person who wants to talk to you on a Webcam starts hinting that a naughty conversation would be a lot of fun. This certainly isn't true for everyone, but if you receive a request out of the blue to chat on a Webcam from someone who you aren't familiar with, then keep in mind that you may be in for something you're not comfortable with. For this reason, you may want to consider being upfront *before* beginning the Webcam conversation that you are not looking for a sexual encounter — unless that is indeed what you are looking for. You don't have to be alarmist or accuse the other person of initiating a Webcam request as a method to see you naked, but instead a simple comment like, "I'd love to chat, as long as that's all we do," or a blatant "Sure, let's chat, but I'm not looking for sex talk" will certainly suffice. This will quickly reveal whether or not the other person was looking for meaningful conversation or was instead looking for something a little more illicit.

Phone Calls

Some dating Web sites offer the option to call people through a telephone system managed by the site. This means that you can call people and listen to messages from them, but you are not directly calling their home phones. The purpose of this feature is to allow singles to reach each other without the need for exchanging home phone numbers. After all, imagine giving a complete stranger your home phone number, talking briefly, and then realizing that there is absolutely no chemistry, only to have this person continue to call you even after you've made it clear that you aren't interested. It not only serves as a safety feature, but also a tool that can help you keep your distance until you truly decide that you want to get to know someone better.

It can be a lot of fun to put a voice to the profile you are interested in, and sometimes it is simply easier to leave a voice message for someone instead of composing a written message. Still, you want to rehearse this message — don't want to wing it. Keep the message brief and to the point, but make sure you let your personality shine through with your voice and that you don't sound like you are reading your message off a piece of paper (even if you are).

Meeting in Person

You have to decide how long you want to wait before you meet someone in person, but if you truly want to meet your match online, then there is a good chance that you will have to meet at least a few people in person before stumbling upon someone who you really click with.

Be aware that you will probably wind up making friends with some of the people you meet face-to-face. You may not click romantically, but you might find the person intriguing, and the feeling might be mutual. This is a bonus of online dating; you get to make friends along the way when trying to find your match.

You're probably not looking for a friendship match; you're looking for a romantic match. For this reason, you're going to have to eventually meet up with the interesting people you correspond with online or speak to over the phone. You won't know if there is a real, valid connection until you actually stand in front of the other person and have a face-to-face conversation.

A full-length mirror can show you things that a partial mirror won't. If you don't have a full length mirror, consider investing in one before your date.

Prepare for the Date

Just because you have chatted with someone online or over the phone, and may feel as though you already know the person, does not mean that you should not make an effort to present a fantastic first impression. You may feel as though the person you have talked to has already fallen in love with you –or at least is attracted to you – and this may make you feel as though you don't have to go through all the regular preparations you would usually go through when getting ready for a first date. For some people, a date with someone they meet online is less like a first date because of all the time they have spent talking and messaging. A face-to-face meeting becomes more like something that is designed to "seal the deal." Instead of thinking of it this way, think of it as the first date with someone who you know a little something about, but is someone you want to impress nonetheless.

Dress attractively and appropriately for the occasion. Don't show up in formal wear if the two of you are heading to a movie, but don't show up wearing sweat pants and a faded T-shirt, either. Think of it in terms of a job interview; you want to dress how the people in the corporation dress, only a little nicer. Do the same thing with your first date; dress how other people will be dressed where you are going, but do something to step it up just a little. It can be something subtle like a spray of cologne or something that takes a little more effort, like getting your hair styled at a salon beforehand. Whatever you choose to wear, and however you decide to present yourself, make sure that you are comfortable. If you're wearing shoes that pinch your feet or if you are wearing something that you feel ridiculous in, chances are your date will pick up on your uncomfortable vibe and may think that it is because you don't find the person attractive or appealing.

Know where you are going. Map out your route to the meeting place far ahead of time so you aren't late for the date. Have a cell phone with you and know the phone number to the place you are going and the cell phone number for the person you are meeting. You want to be able to contact your date in the event that you are running behind schedule, you get a flat tire, or you get lost.

Don't plan on being fashionably late. You may think that it is easier on you to arrive after the person you are meeting because then the burden falls on the other person to find a table or buy tickets or whatever else needs to be done for your date, but the truth is that many people will simply take it as an act of rudeness. Showing up on time (or early) is a sign of respect and anticipation. Showing up late demonstrates that you either don't know how to manage your time or you don't care enough about the first date to make it a priority. Either scenario can be seen as quite undesirable by some.

For this reason, get specific details about where the two of you are meeting. Don't set up something in which you will need to find each other in a crowded place because there is a chance that the two of you may not be able to find each other at all. Don't make plans to meet somewhere that has several similar areas where you might get easily confused. For example, don't plan meet at the trail of a particular park when that park has several different trails. Instead, plan to meet at one specific park, either by name or by location.

If you successfully plan for a date, then this can increase the odds that the two of you will have a good time. A date that starts out with one person arriving late or both people having a hard time finding each other can create a harried tempo that remains throughout the entire date. Avoid this by setting up a pleasant date which you arrive for on time or early, looking great and feeling confident.

Relax!

If you have turned to online dating as a method for meeting people after getting out of a long-term relationship, then you may be a little nervous about the prospect of jumping back into the dating scene. Even if you are active on the dating scene, meeting someone face-to-face can be a little daunting. What if the person does not match up to the image he or she has presented online? What if the person feels that *you* didn't present an accurate portrayal?

Try to relax. The more confident you feel when going into a date with someone you met online, the more relaxed you will be. If you meet someone and bring with you a ton of nervous energy, then this may make the other person feel uneasy. In order to relax before your date, try to think of the things that you use to relax in your everyday life. If stress at work is alleviated by some calming deep breaths, take some time before the date to indulge in some deep breathing. If certain types of music make you feel at ease, listen to that music on your way to the date.

If you feel confident about yourself, it will be easier to relax. There are a variety of ways to feel confident before a date. Making sure that you are dressed in an attractive outfit and that you look well put together can certainly help you feel more confident. If necessary, do some confidence exercises before your date that will help you to feel good about yourself. Try some of these:

- ♥ Write notes to yourself and post them around your home, particularly on mirrors. On the notes, tell yourself that you are a great person, you look good, and that you will have a great time on your date. This is called positive personal affirmations.

- ♥ Stand in front of the mirror and talk to yourself. Tell your reflection that you are fantastic. Talk to yourself about how great a person you are and how great you look. This exercise may feel awkward at first, but it can help if you are having trouble with feeling confident.

♥ Create a mantra that you say to yourself or run through your mind while on your date. It can something as simple as "I look good" or "I'm a fun date." It doesn't have to be something complicated, but refrain from mumbling it to yourself while around other people because this will make you appear a little odd.

You are indeed fantastic! There must be something special about you if the other person wants to make the effort to meet you in person. Take this as a compliment and always keep in mind that you are special and undoubtedly have many positive attributes.

Go Public

No matter how comfortable you feel with someone you meet online, and no matter how great a rapport you develop with the other person through messages and phone calls, it is absolutely imperative that your initial meeting takes place in a public place. This is for your own safety and also to relieve some of the pressure of the first time meeting. In a public venue, such as a coffee shop or a park, there is plenty to see and, consequently, nonstop fodder for conversation.

Meeting at your date's house, or having your date over to your house for the initial meeting, is simply a bad idea. What happens if the two of you don't hit it off? How do you make a graceful exit from your own home? You can't make the claim, "I simply must be getting home" if you're already standing in your kitchen. Worse yet, what if the two of you clash terribly? Do you really want this person to know where you live, or do you want to be stuck at the other person's house if the two of you wind up in an argument? A surefire recipe for disaster is to allow your date to pick you up (so you have no mode of transportation within your own control) and take you to his or her house (so you are on foreign turf while he or she is completely comfortable) and to not tell anyone where you are. Use common sense and try to create a first date that will make you both comfortable, yet give you both ample opportunities to politely exit if it becomes apparent that the two of you just don't mesh well in person.

The Best Locations

There are a few different schools of thought when it comes to picking the best place to have a first time meeting face-to-face with someone you meet online. The best idea is to find a place you both agree on that is public enough to where you won't be alone with someone who is a stranger.

When discussing where to meet, you can either let the other person take the lead or you can make some suggestions. This can be a delicate process. You don't want to appear as though you are insisting upon the places you suggest and blatantly disregarding the suggestions made by the other person. For example, suppose the two of you are talking on the phone and the other person says, "How about we meet at the coffeehouse on 25th Street?" and you shoot back with, "Coffee? I hate coffee. Let's go bowling instead." This certainly is not setting the tone for a good first meeting. In this particular scenario, you may consider meeting at the coffeehouse and getting a tea instead of a coffee, or at least suggesting something else in a more agreeable manner. Using this same example, instead of insisting upon bowling in such a definitive and aggressive way, phrase it to be more of a communal decision instead of something that you insisted upon: "How do you feel about bowling? There is a great bowling alley just down the street from the coffeehouse." You never know; your date may feel the way about bowling that you feel about drinking coffee, so don't force your date to do something that he or she may not enjoy. Making someone engage in an activity that does not appeal to him or her is one way to set the stage for a bad date right from the start.

What type of locations should you suggest? Think of places where you have the best conversations with your friends. Going for coffee has become such a social activity in today's culture. As long as both of you like coffee, it can be a fantastic first date. The environment of most coffee shops is conducive to conversations, with the comfortable seating and the various sites to see within the coffee shop. Drinking a cup of coffee does not take a lot of time, so once the two of you work through your coffee, you can then decide if you want to go for a walk together, order more coffee, see a movie, or maybe even end the date if things just aren't clicking between the two of you.

Meals *can* be a good first date, but it depends largely on whether you feel comfortable eating in front of someone else on a first date (many people don't like eating in front of other people until they really get to know them). Some people avoid meals as first dates because they don't want to deal with an awkward moment when the check comes. They wonder if they should pick up the check, wait for the other person to pick up the check, or if they should whip out their pocket calculator and start dividing the cost straight down the middle. Chances are that most first time dates will probably incur some cost, but nothing is quite so blatant as having the check placed in between the two of you after having a meal. It can be an awkward situation, and "awkward" is not the ambience you are looking for during a first date.

Don't set out to make a date too romantic. The two of you may have hit it off splendidly over the phone and through messages online, but until you meet in person you probably won't know if there is an authentic romantic spark. For this reason, don't set up a first date that is something a couple already in love might do. Stay away from romantic strolls in the park, leisurely walks on the beach, and anything else that does not have a definitive timetable attached to it. Of course, if you start the date at a coffeehouse and then hit it off, there is nothing wrong with extending the date to something a little more intimate. The point is to not set up a first date that does not have a definitive ending, such as the completion of a cup of coffee or the completion of a round of miniature golf. Without a definitive ending, you may have an awkward conclusion to the date.

Try not to schedule a first date that will require a great deal of time. Remember that if the date goes well you can always extend it, but setting up the date to do something that usually takes a few hours may result in an event where you wind up sitting for the last hour wondering what you ever initially saw in this person. Unless you are an avid fan, don't agree to attend a baseball game. An evening benefit that lasts for a few hours is not the best first date. A dinner cruise that extends out to a sightseeing venture may be a lot of fun, but it can also be torture if you realize early on in the evening that you really don't mesh well with the other person.

Suggest something that will give you both something to do as well as give you a way to either extend the date or call the date to an end early. Meet for dessert at a low-key bakery. Meet for drinks at a local pub. Whatever you do, stay flexible and make it is something you will both enjoy. The worst-case scenario is you find you don't like each other in the least and you end the date quickly. But the best-case scenario is that the date you plan turns out to be merely an introduction to a fantastic evening with someone you get along with really well.

Reflect on the Date

Chances are, you will already be mulling over the events of the date even before you say goodbye to the other person. If the two of you aren't clicking, you may be wondering if the other person realizes that there is no spark. And if the two of you are getting along really well, then you may be wondering (and hoping) if the other person feels the same spark. Try not to let your internal ruminations ruin the date. You may think you're simply mulling over everything that's going on, but your date might come to the conclusion that you are introverted, shy, or just not into the date at all. Take your time to ponder what's working and what isn't, but try not to let it get in the way of interacting with your date.

The time to really reflect on the date is after the date is over and you have already returned home. This is the time to mull over everything that happened and to decide if there is a chance that this person is right for you. You don't have to get incredibly meticulous in this analysis — spreadsheets and long lists of pros and cons aren't necessary unless you actually enjoy doing this sort of thing — but you should reflect on the date and figure what worked and what didn't. If you spend an extended period of time with online dating, then the odds are that you will go on several face-to-face dates with the people you meet online.

For this reason, reflecting on the dates you have will only help you with future dates. Ask yourself questions like "What worked with this date?" and "What didn't work with this date?" The experiences you have with dates early on may dictate the way you plan future dates. Maybe you will find a favorite spot where you like to meet people for the first time, or maybe after getting stuck with the check, you decide that you will never suggest a dinner date ever again. Experiences can be great ways of knowing what to plan for future dates and how to handle yourself on those dates.

With some people, you will get an immediate epiphany that this is not the person for you. It may be that you don't have similar morals and beliefs, you think the person is crass and rude, or it may just be that the two of you don't mesh well as individuals. Whatever the reason, accept the epiphany as a gift from your subconscious, and don't try to see the person again. You don't have to be rude about not wanting to see someone again, but don't allow your desire to follow social graces force you into agreeing to another date. Remember: With online dating, there are *always* more fish in the sea. You don't have to endure future dates with people who you know you don't want to actually have a relationship with. Save both of you the time and trouble and don't agree (or suggest) another date if you know there is really no point.

Reconnecting

How long should you wait before you contact the other person after your date has ended? If the two of you hit it off really well, then there is nothing wrong with a quick e-mail or text that says, "Thanks again for the date, I had a great time!" However, you probably don't want to pick up the phone and call the same person who you just said goodbye to 20 minutes ago. If you want to see the person again, and if the two of you did not set concrete plans to see each other again, call or send a message the next day to find out when the two of you can get together again.

It's a delicate balance. You don't want to appear needy and obsessive, but on the other hand, you don't want to seem so aloof that you turn the other person off. Imagine if you had a great date with someone and then you didn't hear from that person for several days. You try contacting the person a couple of times, and when the two of you finally connect, the excuse you receive from the other person is, "Oh, I've been so busy." Frankly, unless the person has a job that takes him or her to faraway places or is sitting in the hospital room of a dying friend, there is no reason why he or she can't pick up the phone or send a quick message. It's an insult to ignore messages and other attempts at contact, even if it is all done in an attempt to stay calm and cool over someone new.

Treat people how you would like to be treated when it comes to contacting them after a date. If you never want to see someone again, don't string the person along because you don't feel comfortable insulting him or her. If you want to see someone again, don't be shy about expressing your hopes for another date. Honesty is the best policy, but just don't go overboard. Don't send a text two minutes after you leave your date that says, "I think I'm in love with you!" By the same token, don't send a text two minutes after you leave your date that says, "You are a pig and I never want to see you again." Either way, you're presenting a potentially scary persona.

CASE STUDY: MELANIE'S STORY

"I started dating online in 2002, shortly after I broke up with my boyfriend of five years. What an adventure that turned out to be! I met all kinds of guys, some really nice, but with no chemistry (at least not from my end), and some that I really liked, but who turned out to be real jerks!

There was one guy I met that appeared to be a very successful businessman...and on our first date, he took me to a lovely restaurant and we enjoyed a great evening. Unfortunately, on the next date we had, after dinner, and without telling me, he drove me to his house, which I was not very comfortable with. He was then quizzing me whether I could see spending the rest of my life with him — I had just met him, for Pete's sake! That was the end of that, but it made me very nervous how much he rushed things and didn't tell me we were going to his house.

Then, there was the ever-so-charming 'Tom,' who had a great sense of humor and who I definitely hit it off with. But he came on like gangbusters as far as wanting to spend time together, planning something to do every day of the weekend and some weeknights. This went on for about two weeks, until one Saturday night, in the middle of our date, he decided that we were 'spending too much time together,' so he stopped the date mid-stream and dropped me off at home. That was the end of Tom! I broke it off the next day — too weird for me. (Although, strangely, we ended up in touch again a few months later and developed a friendship that continues to this day).

One person I met, whose name I can't even remember at this point, was great via e-mail and over the phone. We had so much in common. I was even open-minded to the fact that he had children (and I don't). Then, when we met for lunch, nearly the first thing he said to me was, 'I didn't realize you would be so voluptuous. I prefer women to be more like a size four.' I felt like saying 'And I didn't realize you would be so shallow and small-minded!' That was fine with me because I didn't find any chemistry with him, but I was, of course, quite insulted. I had not misrepresented myself. I'm very athletic and I stated that in my profile, not to mention I had plenty of photos. Go figure!

Then, there was the yacht captain who I had two great dates with, right before he had to go on a boat trip for about 10 days. He actually called me one time from the yacht and had mentioned when he should be returning and said he wanted to get together when he got back. That time came and went, and when I tried calling him (after not hearing from him), a woman ended up answering his phone. I finally got an e-mail from him that he decided he liked the concept of me more than he actually liked me. I still haven't figured out what that one meant.

And then came Scott, and I hit it off with him so well. He had a great sense of humor; we were both in the technology field and loved animals. I was giddy after

CASE STUDY: MELANIE'S STORY

our first date, and we had an amazing second date where we went bowling. He told me it had been a long time since he'd felt like this for someone, and I felt the same way. Well, after a few weeks we became intimate, and a few days after that, when I felt like something wasn't quite right, he told me that he still wanted to see me, but that he also wanted to see another girl he had been speaking to online around the time he met me. I, of course, said no, because in my book you don't date other people after you've been intimate, and that one really stung because I could have really fallen for him. It wasn't meant to be.

After kissing so many frogs and other undesirable creatures, I was of course gun-shy when I met Graham. I had actually taken my **www.Match.com** profile down for a few weeks; I was so tired of it all. For some reason, I made my profile active again. Graham's profile came to me in an e-mail as a potential match. His picture didn't compel me that much because I didn't like blondes, but I did like his profile (He described himself as a smashing Englishman who loved to dance, which I found out later was not exactly the truth). I didn't even bother e-mailing him, but sent him a "wink". He e-mailed me back.

I usually had very high standards about how someone's writing should be in e-mail, being an English major and a writer myself. His e-mail wasn't great, but I'd been dating for so long, I just told him to call me on the phone to cut to the chase, and I had pretty much forgot about him, as I ended up meeting someone 'the old-fashioned' way, while out with some friends. I had a date scheduled with Luis for that Friday night and got stood up! So, I made other plans to go downtown with a girlfriend.

That's when Graham ended up calling me. We hit it off right away on the phone and when it was getting to be time for me to go, I asked Graham how spontaneous he was, and if he'd like to continue our conversation downtown. He agreed and came out to meet me. We hit it off famously in-person as well.

I was nervous because he told me some of the same things other guys had told me as well, that they wanted a relationship or that they could see us together. However, in his case, he was genuine and really did mean it! We were pretty much together ever since that first night we met downtown.

We got married eight months later, and we're about to celebrate four happy years (and we just found out we're pregnant)! Oh, and one other side note: I was the very first girl he met in person from Match.com."

Ten Dating Tips for Women

1. Do not mention your biological clock, your desire to have children in the next year, or that you are ready to settle down. This can be a fast way to scare a man off.

2. Do not brag about being a sex goddess. Better yet, do not talk about sex at all.

3. No matter how agonizingly slow the minutes are crawling by, do not check your watch constantly.

4. Do not order the veal chop, the New York strip steak, the butter-braised lobster, or the most expensive bottle of wine available. In the same vein, do not order a side salad and sneak fries off his plate.

5. Do not talk about your workout regimen, strict diet, makeup, manicure, outfit, hairstyle, or anything related to vanity and insecurity. Make him think you look good without any effort.

6. Do not run off to the bathroom every five minutes. Either you will make him think you have a serious bladder problem, you are so vain that you cannot go five minutes without looking at yourself, or you are trying desperately to get away.

7. Do not whip out your compact and touch up your mascara, powder your nose, or fix your hair.

8. Never, ever talk about your thunder thighs, your double chin, or any other body part. Maybe he did not even notice; maybe he likes it. Do yourself a favor and do not call attention to your perceived flaws.

9. Do not tell him you never kiss on the first date and then agree to go home with him.

10. Do not forget to thank him for the date and tell him that you had a great time.

Ten Dating Tips for Men

1. Do not comment on how she eats, whether she is picking at a salad or heartily enjoying a rack of lamb. You should feel content that she is somewhat comfortable enough to eat in front of you in the first place.

2. Do not tell her that she should grow her bangs out, let her hair grow, lose some weight, gain some weight, or make any alterations to her physical appearance whatsoever. A girl wants to feel as though you like her as is.

3. Do not bring her a bouquet of flowers, buy her a rose, or bring her any other small token. While you may think it is romantic, she may be embarrassed because she has to carry it around all night long.

4. Do not make any negative comments about clothing, whether it is in regard to not understanding why

women have so many articles of clothing or her outfit of choice. Women do not take clothing lightly; she could have changed ten times before making a decision.

5. Do not wait until the last minute to make plans. This makes her think you did not care enough to arrange something ahead of time.

6. Do not pick the restaurant and proceed to complain about paying for valet parking, coat check, and the price of the entrees.

7. Do not be late. She will not appreciate having to sit alone at the bar waiting for you. Always be at least ten minutes early.

8. Have a woman or a friend who knows something about clothes critique your choice of outfit. Pay particular attention to your shoes and to mixing a brown belt with black shoes and vice versa. Like it or not, she may make a mental note about your choice of clothing.

9. Do not look anywhere other than your date's face when she is speaking. Her eyes are on her face, not in her shirt. Make eye contact.

10. Do not act like God's gift to women. She will not appreciate your arrogance, your cockiness, or your attitude. Let her see how good of a catch you are; do not tell her.

Ten Dating Tips for Everyone

1. Do not spend too much time talking about yourself. Instead, ask questions and answer accordingly. Do not launch into a 20-minute diatribe to answer the question, "How was your day?"

2. Do not air out your dirty laundry, give out too much information, over-share, or whatever else you want to call it. This means talking about your vulnerabilities, insecurities, baggage, hang-ups, skeletons, secrets, and the like.

3. Turn off your cell phone. If you do it when you go to a movie theater, do it when on a date — no matter where the date is taking place.

4. Do not complain about how all the good ones are taken, how hard it is to find a date, or how you have been single for so long. In other words, do not make any complaints, general or specific, about dating.

5. Under no circumstances should you make any references to your exes. This should be quite obvious.

6. It is unwise to go on a date if you are sick. It does not matter if you have a cold, a headache, the flu, or you are nauseous; reschedule. If you do not do so, you risk being miserable, making your date think he or she is the reason you are miserable, and making your date sick.

7. Exercise some restraint and do not drink so much that you get sick or pass out. It is incredibly off-putting, but also incredibly unsafe. You do not know the person you are out with; how can you be sure he or she will not take advantage of you?

8. Do not continuously ask your date if you look all right, if you are dressed appropriately, if you ordered the right thing, or if your choice of venue is acceptable. Read: Do not constantly seek reassurance and act insecure.

9. Do not make fun of anyone for any reason and do not make any racist or sexist comments. You do not know what the other person's views are on these things, and you certainly do not want to risk offending or alienating him or her.

10. Put your blinders on and avoid looking at, staring at, or checking out anyone else. Your date will not appreciate this in any way, shape, or form.

Above all else, *be yourself* and try your best to have a good time!

CASE STUDY: MICHAEL AND RACHEL'S STORY

This success story appears courtesy of
www.AmericanSingles.com.

Dear AmericanSingles.com,

When a single computer geek decides he wants to find love, it isn't long before he realizes that he can't write a nifty computer program to reach his goal. Being a computer geek myself, I'm quite sure of this fact! After a small handful of mismatches in the "traditional" dating world, I tried my hand online and chose AmericanSingles. I logged on and created what I was sure was a relatively disinteresting profile under the name kahzmo8857. I paid for three months of a Premium Membership, figuring it would take at least that long to figure it all out.

That same day, I found her. She was beautiful! That smile! That profile! So sweet and confident! ...So out of my league! Her name was 30151659. Oh yes, I wanted 30151659 to be mine! I sent her a message and hoped she would respond. Little did I know that her Premium Membership had expired, but upon receiving notification that she had a message waiting, figured she'd check it out and renew her Premium Membership for another three months to read what I had written. Thank God! She responded right then and there.

We spoke briefly by instant messenger and found instant chemistry. She was hilarious and fun! She typed "haha" to my poorly timed jokes. She made a *Star Wars* reference. Had I found my perfect geek match?

We set our first date for the very next evening. She told me her name... Rachel. I love her name! When I picked her up, my emotions were mixed. She was even more beautiful in person. That was a good thing, but it also made me believe even more that she was way out of my league, and the nervous jitters set in. Despite my nervousness, we had a fun, pleasant evening and chatted non-stop over dinner. We were very different. I enjoyed computer programming, the Internet, and camping. She enjoyed NASCAR, Angels baseball, and dancing. We were not the same, but somehow that was OK with both of us. It just seemed to work. After a little over one week and one date from AmericanSingles, we canceled our Premium Memberships.

We dated again and again, and then again. Within two weeks, we were inseparable. When we realized we were falling in love, we were excited. With no conscious effort on our part, our lives began to merge from two separate lives into one life together. Months later, we were living together.

CASE STUDY: MICHAEL AND RACHEL'S STORY

We were both products of divorced and single parents, and we were both overcome with how happy we had become. Neither of us had felt this way before. We found the real thing; we found true love. And there was no way it would have happened had it not been for AmericanSingles.

After six months together, I asked Rachel to marry me. She said yes! My dreams had come true!

As we plan our lives together and work on raising a family as husband and wife, we will forever be grateful to AmericanSingles for bringing us together. We've discussed it at length, and we are both positive that the circumstances were such that we never would have met had it not been for your site. We owe you more than three months' worth of membership fees.

Thank you so much from the bottom of our hearts. From Rachel and me, our kids, our future kids, and our extended family, we thank you for bringing us a lifetime of joy. You changed our lives! Bless you!

With kind regards,

Michael and Rachel
Simi Valley, California

CHAPTER 9

Cautions

While it is certainly true that you can meet the love of your life online, it is also unfortunately true that you may encounter some people who are out to scam you or who are not really who they say they are. It isn't difficult to create a false persona online. It is entirely possible to create a character designed to be the person the creator wants to be or to be someone who is appealing to people who have a great deal of money.

Keep in mind that even though it's possible to encounter someone online who is out to scam you, it is not the norm. The majority of online daters are people just like you who are simply trying to meet some new people and potentially fall in love. You don't need to enter the realm of online dating with a high dose of skepticism or fear, but instead, remember that you won't truly know if people are indeed who they say they are until you have a chance to meet them and get to know them. Don't be terrified that someone is only out to steal your identity, but don't assume that everyone is exactly who they say they are, either.

Little White Lies

Some online daters aren't who they say they are, but don't necessarily intentionally set out to craft a false profile out of malicious intent. Instead, these people either have a warped sense of self or have inflated their positive attributes and minimized the negative in an attempt to make themselves desirable. For example, a woman who is overweight may simply categorize herself with a body type of "a few extra pounds" when instead — if she wanted to present a realistic portrayal of herself — should list herself as "heavy" or even "big and beautiful." Maybe she does not actually realize how heavy she truly is, or perhaps she figures that she carries herself well so nobody would ever guess her true weight. In a situation like this, it is obvious that she isn't out to defraud anyone, even though she is not telling the whole truth.

While little white lies are a concern when dating online, they should not set out a bunch of red flags that the other person is trying to swindle you. For example, if a man's profile picture features him with a hat, and he neglects to tell you that he is completely bald — which you, of course, abruptly realize on your first face-to-face meeting — this is not justification for you to run for the hills out of fear that this man is trying to get his hands on your bank account. Perhaps he's incredibly embarrassed about his baldness, or on the other hand, maybe he never mentioned it because it's just not a big deal to him. Either way, these small lies and omissions are not the type of things that should have you panicked over online dating.

The Clues

What type of things should you be vigilant about? Although there is no definitive way to spot a crook within an online dating base, there are signs that perhaps something is not quite right with someone and should tip you off that you should use extreme caution or cease contact altogether.

The Model's Photo

The only people who should have online dating profiles that make them look like models are models. In other words, if a profile photo looks eerily like a model's headshot but isn't attached to a profile of a person who claims to do modeling work, then you can assume that the photo does not actually belong to the person or is likely highly doctored. Either scenario is a tip-off that something is not quite right about the person.

It is not hard to get access to a stock photo of a model. Web sites like **www.iStockphoto.com** and stock.xchng® allow users to download photos of people, often at no charge. Not all of these photos available for download look posed or feature incredibly attractive people. In fact, it is possible to find a photograph of a completely average-looking person online and download it to an online dating profile. Most of the people who view the profile will not even think twice about the photo being fake.

For this reason, if a glance at the profile photo gives you pause, ask yourself what it is about the photo that seems wrong to you. If it seems as though the picture just looks too posed, or if you are convinced that the picture is of a model as opposed to someone simply posting an online dating profile, then you have three choices: You can ignore the iffy feeling you have about the photo, you can ask the person about the photo, or you can decide that you'll trust your gut instinct and cease contact with the person. Many would argue that it is always best to trust your gut instinct, so unless there is something incredibly intriguing about this person and everything else seems legitimate, it may be time to move on.

The Sob Story

Say you meet someone online and immediately click. The person has a lot of the same interests and passions as you do and genuinely seems interested and eager to get to know you better. The two of you don't meet immediately because of scheduling conflicts or whatever else keeps you apart, but you spend plenty of time chatting online and talking on the phone.

Before long you receive a message from this person. Things are not going well, the person reveals. Something has happened and the person has fallen into an unforeseen financial emergency. It may be that the person's car has broken down, the person just found out that there is an urgent need for a costly medical procedure, or maybe the person is about to get evicted. Whatever the claim, the situation usually involves a sense of urgency and desperation that is designed to elicit a response from you that includes an offer of financial assistance.

It is entirely possible for these situations to occur and be completely legitimate, but there is a better chance that the person is merely trying to get money out of you. People like this may juggle more than one online relationship concurrently that all wind up with requests for money. People who create this type of online scam do so in the hopes that they can create a connection with some people and then make an appeal for some money. After the money is received, these people either disappear or stick around in order to ask for more money. Don't fall for this! Even if a request for money is completely genuine based on a real and valid situation, it is generally not a good idea to give money to someone you hardly know. The best case scenario is that this is a person who really needs the money, but will be understanding that you are not willing or able to open your wallet. The worst case scenario is that this person is a scam artist who will take you for a great deal of money before you realize you have been scammed.

Make it a rule to never give money to anyone you meet online. No matter how authentic the request seems, or how dire the situation the other person paints the picture to be, this should be one rule that you don't break. Refusing to give money to the people you meet online will protect you from potentially bad situations and will additionally weed out the potential mates who aren't interested in anything beyond the material things you can give them.

Again, let common sense be your guide. Chances are you will never encounter anyone who wants anything other than to meet some new people and maybe meet someone special.

Dangerous Liaisons

Another area where you should use common sense is when it comes to actually meeting someone face-to-face. The rules for a first date with someone you meet online are no different from a blind date with someone you've never met before. Always meet in a public place. Make sure someone else knows where you are and who you are with. Don't leave the public place to go somewhere private with the other person.

It is a good idea to keep personal information to yourself initially, such as where you live or where you work. You don't want to present information to other people online that can be pieced together to reveal a way to find you for a face-to-face meeting that you aren't prepared for. It isn't even that you necessarily have to fear that someone will stalk you or try to find you with the intent of doing you harm, but you don't want to reveal so much about yourself (the block you live on, the church you attend, the college you take evening classes at) that you might find yourself bumping into the same person from the online dating site that you decided you didn't want to meet.

Revealing too much about yourself can also open you up to identity theft. A person does not necessarily have to meet you in person in order to steal your identity. If you give enough personal information, then it may be all an identity thief needs to open up a credit account in your name. Be particularly wary if someone finds a way to ask about your birth date, your mother's maiden name, or the name of the financial institution where you keep your accounts. You may be surprised at how these topics can ease their way into conversation without seeming like odd questions at all.

"I see you're an Aries; are you right on the cusp? What is your actual birthday?"

"You look like you have German ancestry. What was your mom's last name before she got married? Was it a German name?"

"I am so mad at my bank right now because of all these fees they keep piling on my account. Where do you have your checking account? Maybe I should switch to your bank if you're happy with the service there."

These all seem like typical bits of conversation, but when pieced together it may be enough information to get someone started on the road to stealing your identity. *This does not mean everyone asking these types of questions is trying to steal your identity.* Don't wind up so frightened at the prospect of someone wishing you ill will that you panic whenever you are asked a question that may or may not be used to cause you trouble.

Any time you are asked a question that you don't want to answer — for whatever reason — simply state that you don't want to answer the question or instead change the subject. Only get suspicious when the person keeps pressing you for an answer to something that you know you should not respond to.

The Players and the Users

If you're trying online dating in an attempt to hook up with random people, then you probably won't mind that there are some people online who are only out for one-night stands. On the other hand, if you are looking to meet your match online, then you need to be aware that there are some people online who are absolutely *not* looking for love, but may masquerade as someone genuinely looking for a soul mate in order to gain access to singles through a dating site.

There are plenty of Web sites online that cater to singles (and married people) who only want a brief sexual encounter. Stay away from those sites unless this is what you want as well.

How can you tell if someone is pretending to want a serious relationship, but really only wants to get you in bed? Truth be told, some people in this position try to convince themselves that they are truly ready for a committed relationship, but in reality, they aren't ready at all. They may figure that at their age it's time to settle down and start a family, or maybe they think they're ready for marriage, but in reality, have not yet healed the emotional scars from previous relationships. For this reason, you should realize that not all people who merely want a sexual encounter will be easy to spot. After all, if they don't even know that they don't actually want a relationship, how are you supposed to glean this information from their profiles?

There are blatant signs that someone simply wants a quick sexual encounter. Some of these people come on entirely too strong, too early. The beginning stages of the initial conversations may be normal enough, but the topic will quickly become sexual and may even reach a point where the person is urging you to participate in phone sex or meet up somewhere for a sexual encounter. For people looking to meet the loves of other lives, this is not common behavior.

Pay attention to a person's profile. If the photos are all suggestive, or if the profile text is full of innuendos, then there is a good chance that this person is more concerned with having sex than meeting someone and cultivating a meaningful and loving relationship.

Slow Down

Yes, you can meet someone special online, and yes, you may even meet the love of your life online. It is unlikely, however, that you will stumble upon your true love's profile and immediately know that this is the person you want to spend the rest of your life with. Just like with any other type of relationship, the relationships you form with the people you meet while dating online will have to be cultivated and nurtured.

For this reason, you should be a little apprehensive if someone you just met online starts insinuating that the two of you are meant to be together. It is one thing to recognize that you two are a good match and that you have plenty of things in common, but it's another thing entirely to announce that it's love at first sight. You want people to find you appealing and attractive, but you don't want to become someone's obsession.

For example, suppose you contact someone online after a compatibility tool matches the two of you as suitable for each other. You trade messages back and forth, then spend all night on the phone talking to each other. You feel like there is a real connection, and you look forward to meeting the person face-to-face in the near future. The next morning, there is a message from your new potential mate, and when you click to open it, you're stunned to see that it's a declaration of love. Apparently, the other person is completely smitten by you, has never felt this strongly about anyone so quickly, and wants to marry you. You're wondering if you may feel the same way.

Slow down. No matter how compatible you feel as though the two of you may be, it is highly unlikely that you can fall in love with someone via a couple of computer messages and a lengthy phone call. You need to meet someone face-to-face before you can decide whether or not there is real potential for love there.

What do you do when someone else decides that you are the perfect match, but you don't feel that way at all? The beauty of online dating — and of not revealing too much private information in the beginning stages of getting to know someone — is the fact that you can simply disappear from the other person's screen. Although it is true that this may not be the most polite way to go about ending communications, it certainly comes in handy when you're getting a creepy vibe from someone who insists the two of you are meant to be together.

It is unlikely that you are going to genuinely fall in love with someone online in a day or two, just like it is highly unlikely that someone else is going to genuinely fall in love with you within the same time span. If your goal is to meet your match online, think of it as a process instead of something that is going to happen instantaneously. If you feel like you're in love, give yourself time to really examine your feelings (and, of course, to actually meet the other person face-to-face to see if the amorous feelings still remain), and if another online single tells you that he or she is in love with you, then you should do the same thing. Finding your match online is not a race; it's a process.

Just Plain Mean

Although it is unlikely, you may indeed encounter some online singles who become mean, inappropriate, or abusive in their correspondence to you. If this does happen, most Web sites have procedures that are in place that allow you to report the abusive person to the administrators of the site. Depending on the rules and regulations of the site, and if your claims can be substantiated, the administrators may then cancel the other person's membership and erase the profile.

If you run into a situation where someone is harassing you online through a dating Web site, then check the terms of usage on the site and find out what you need to do to report the person. Keep in mind that some sites may assume no responsibility for policing the site, while other sites may have very stringent guidelines that spell out what happens to people who do not adhere to the code of conduct set forth by the site. Report the harassment using the proper procedure dictated by the site. Some sites may require copies of the harassing messages, while others may simply accept a summary from you with regards to what it going on. Just be sure to find out what the site requires for a formal complaint so you don't have to repeat the process several times.

These procedures *are not* in place to punish people who don't respond to your correspondence, people who tell you they aren't interested in you, or people who annoy you when you talk on the phone or meet in-person. This is not a method that should be used in an attempt to gain retribution from someone who insults you in an unintentional way, such as by jokingly making fun of East Coast people after you mention you were born in New York. Dating Web sites with these procedures in place do so because they are trying to protect members from malicious messages and other harassment from unscrupulous people trolling the sites.

When should you consider reporting someone's bad behavior? You should refer to the code of conduct of the site you are using, but in general, there are a few situations which always merit a note to the administrators of the dating site. For example, if a member sends you sexually explicit notes or photographs (which you did not request, nor do you appreciate), this is something you should report. If a member blatantly insults you or threatens you, this should be reported. If you stumble upon a profile that contains highly offensive text or photographs, this is something that should be reported unless you're using a dating site designed for people who want to place explicit items within their profiles and are encouraged to do so.

If you truly feel threatened by someone else online through a dating site, and if that person knows where you live, work, or can otherwise find you, then this is a matter that should be brought to local law enforcement authorities. Although laws vary by region, the person sending threatening messages to you may be committing a crime. Be sure to also report this to the administrators of the dating site so they can remove this person from the site and maybe prevent the person from harassing anyone else within the database.

Your Public Profile

Your online profile is probably going to be read by many other singles. That's good news because the wider you cast your net, the more likely you will catch the eye of potentially compatible people. On the other hand, it may not only be eligible singles who peruse your profile. If your profile is publicly accessible, then you're allowing just about anyone to have a look to see how you present yourself.

Even if you don't use your real name, you may be surprised at how easily people can stumble upon your profile. A quick search of your geographic area can lead someone right to your profile, so anyone who knows you have a profile online can find you with enough effort. Even if you join a dating Web site that does not feature a database that is accessible to non-members, in most cases, it does not take much for a person to gain access to the database using an introductory registration or by going through an acquaintance who is already registered on the site.

This does not mean that your profile is going to be so incredibly accessible that an Internet search under your name will yield a direct link to your profile. Just keep in mind that by posting an online dating profile, you are indeed making your search for your match a public affair to a certain extent.

For this reason, carefully consider the items you place on your profile. Don't spend half a paragraph lamenting about how crazy your parents are because you never know if the information will eventually wind up in front of your parents. Don't blast your ex-spouse on your profile as an abusive moron, because not only is this tacky and a potential turn-off among the other singles on the site, but if it gets back to your ex-spouse, it could turn into a big issue. Online dating does not afford you a great deal of anonymity, even if it *feels* anonymous without the face-to-face contact.

Think about what your employer — or potential employer — might read in your profile. If you spend a portion of your profile revealing that you hate your job and that you would give just about anything to quit, then you shouldn't be entirely shocked if you eventually find yourself sitting in your boss' office, explaining why you are posting such lamentations online. This is doubly true if your dating site of choice is additionally a social networking site like Facebook or MySpace because these sites are easily accessible when privacy features aren't in place. Even when these additional features are in place, there is always a chance that one of your "friends" with access to your page can forward your comments directly to your boss or whoever else you blast on your profile.

Potential employers sometimes conduct online searches for information for prospective employers. This is becoming increasingly common. Sometimes it is an internal employee who conducts the search, and sometimes it's a third party specializing in pulling up "dirt" on people who are being considered for a position. Think about it: If you were the principal of a school, would you want to hire a new teacher whose online dating profile was filled with sexual innuendos or criticisms?

While you don't want to censor yourself to the point where you aren't presenting a realistic portrayal, you also don't want to be so frank and open that the things you put on your dating profile get you into trouble. Think of your profile as a brief introduction to who you are. You want to present a summary, but you don't want to reveal everything. It's like the back cover on a novel: A summary is presented that will intrigue people to read the book, but not so much is revealed that readers don't even need to open the pages of the book in order to get the full spectrum of the story.

CASE STUDY: JUNE'S STORY

"My boss was a real jerk. He always made everyone think he was so conservative and religious, but then the male employees would come up to me and say that they swore he was hitting on them, like he would put his arm around them and stuff like that. None of us could prove that he was hitting on them, and the bosses above him dismissed all the claims because he was considered a real stand-up guy in the community.

So I decided to take things into my own hands and prove that he was hiding something. We shared a computer at work, so one day when he was out at lunch I looked up the Internet history and found that he was spending time on a chat site called Worlds Chat. It was a chat room where you picked an avatar and then 'walked around' in different rooms and talked to people. Everyone I knew who used that site used it to try to meet people to hook up.

I was able to find his avatar's name really easily because he had the computer set to automatically fill in the information when the Web site first came up, so after I knew his avatar's name, I waited until I knew he was on the computer and I ran to my friend's desk and had him log on to the site. We created an avatar and went looking for my boss in the online chat world. We found him pretty quickly and struck up a conversation, and it wasn't long before he was totally hitting on our male avatar! He started saying all sorts of dirty things, and we were so stunned that we logged off and just sat there looking at each other for a minute before deciding to keep this experience to ourselves because we were just plain horrified. I think the moral of the story is that even when you think something is totally anonymous, it isn't."

CHAPTER 10

You Change, Your Needs Change

After you have been involved with online dating for a while, you may find that you look back on your early experiences feeling as though you have learned quite a bit throughout your time as an online dater. As you learn more about the process of online dating, you'll quickly find that there are better ways of doing certain things and approaching certain singles. There are some people who spend a year or two dating online before they either meet someone special or eventually decide to stop dating online.

You need to be ready and willing to make changes when they are needed. Whether this mean updating your profile with new wording or different photographs, or switching the Web site you utilize for your online dating, you should think of your online dating experience as an evolving process. Unless you meet someone great quickly — which certainly *does* happen sometimes — then you may find yourself revising your profile and approach on a regular basis.

Periodically Review Your Needs

You want to regularly review a few things. Think of it as a marketing experiment: What type of responses do you get when you portray yourself in one way as opposed to portraying yourself in another way? Are you attracting the type of people you are actually interested in? If you notice a trend in the type of people who initiate contact based on your profile, think about what prompts these types of people to find you appealing. For example, if you seem to be attracting more than your share of people who are highly religious and conservative — and this isn't really what you are looking for — then you may want to review the level of importance that you initially placed on a match's level of religious involvement. Perhaps you need to phrase it more as a spirituality issue than one that pertains to a certain religion or political affiliation.

If you find yourself scratching your head, wondering why you are attracting the types of people who are contacting you, then have someone else take a look at your profile and give you an honest review of what type of person you are portraying. This should give you the information you need in order to make the necessary adjustments so you can present a more accurate portrayal and attract the kind of people you are actually interested in dating.

Your profile review is not just something you do when you are first preparing to post your profile to a dating Web site. Instead, it's an ongoing process in which you periodically review your profile. Your knowledge and understanding of online dating is going to increase exponentially as you grow accustomed to the way things work, so it only makes sense that you take the time once in a while to make sure that your profile isn't contrary to the things you've learned. For example, if after being involved with online dating for a couple of weeks, you realize that you get absolutely annoyed when people use smileys within the text of their profile page — but then review your own profile page and realize that you also inserted a smiley here and there — this will reveal that maybe it's time to rewrite some portions of your profile.

Correspondence

Your online dating profile is not the only thing that needs to be reviewed once in a while to make sure it is accurate. It is important to also occasionally review the way you initiate conversations with singles as well as the method you use to respond to people who initiate contact with you.

While you may want to personalize every correspondence you send out in an attempt to get to know someone a little better, there is a good chance that you may find yourself writing a similar note to everyone. These initial contacts can get a little formulaic after a while, especially if you send out a large amount of them at once. Pay close attention to what type of reaction you get to the things you say in these notes. Do people respond rapidly and favorably, or do they respond with luke-warm reactions or not respond at all? Although you have to remember that there is not one perfect note that is guaranteed to elicit a response from every single person you contact, you will begin to notice a pattern that there may be certain things you say that always seem to get a response of some kind. If it's the kind of response you are looking for, then you're doing something right.

Review everything before you hit send. Whether it is running a note through a spellchecker or reading it aloud to yourself so you can hear how it flows, a quick review of whatever you're sending can save you from accidentally saying something that you didn't mean to say. Your reviews should be two-fold: one quick review for everything you send out, and periodic reviews that help you to make sure you are getting responses of the caliber you are seeking.

You should also review the other methods you use to initiate contact. If you prefer sending quick "flirts" or "pokes" to other singles as a first introduction, figure out if this is indeed the best method to use. How many people respond to these initial contacts, and is the response favorable? Some people do not like these little contacts because they are slightly ambiguous and do nothing more than say something along the lines of, "Hi, I was looking at your profile, and you look interesting, and now I'm putting the ball into your court." If this method does not yield the type of results you are looking for, it may be time to switch things up and to start sending some written notes instead of using the flirts and pokes.

CASE STUDY: MARJORIE'S STORY

"I was recently divorced and decided to try the on-line dating site **www.Match.com**. The ad was on my e-mail every single day. I filled out the information and set up payment. One of the first responses I had to my profile was from someone who only responded once and then disappeared. I did not hear from him again – or so I thought.

After getting responses from some other users, I went on a few dates. Mostly I had lunch or dinner with someone once and then did not hear from them again. That was OK. The response was mostly mutual.

I had not heard from the first person who responded to my profile for a few months. I had pretty much forgotten. Then, he got in touch a second time. We lived about 70 miles apart, but I traveled to the city where he lived weekly to visit family. I suggested that we meet for coffee or lunch, but he declined and then was out of town for a few weeks. Again, I heard nothing.

Soon, he contacted me again and we continued to e-mail. He sounded good in the e-mails, but I figured that we should meet face-to-face to find out if there was still some interest. We arranged to meet for lunch on Monday, February 17, 2003. I had a holiday from my job and was going to visit my mother after my lunch date. Because I was not familiar with the restaurant where he wanted to have lunch, we arranged to meet at an exit and then I followed him in my own car. (I thought it was always better to be in my own vehicle when I was meeting a date for the first time. I always had an escape route.)

When I first saw Bill I thought, 'Oh, he's too cute for me!' I thought he might not be interested, but I could not back out and I thought that I would never know if I didn't at least have a meal with him. I followed him to the restaurant, figuring that this would be another one-time encounter.

I was so impressed with his manners and consideration right from the start. Although we have very different backgrounds and professions, we were able to talk very easily through the entire meal. Bill was ready to get to know me and to

CASE STUDY: MARJORIE'S STORY

let me get to know him. I was very impressed with his intelligence and his devotion to his family. He was recently widowed and talked very affectionately about his three adult daughters, two of whom lived nearby.

Even after one meeting, I knew that Bill was special. I cut off contact with any of the other men I had communicated with through Match.com.

We kept in touch over the next days by telephone and e-mail. I again traveled to his city in a week or so after our first meeting. We met again for coffee. This time, I had a friend with me. She was also impressed by Bill's looks and manner.

Bill and I have basically been together ever since that first meeting. We saw each other as often as possible for two years. Then we were married on December 10, 2005.

We comment to each other nearly every day that we are enormously fortunate to have each other as friend, spouse, and lover."

Your Needs

Maybe when you first started getting involved with online dating, you thought that you were looking for someone who lives within your city limits and who is as passionate about baseball as you are, but then after meeting and dating a few people who fall into this category, you decide that maybe you need to change what you are looking for. Maybe you don't meet anyone who matches the standards you set and decide to loosen the standards so that you can discover who else is out there. Whatever the reason, you need to be aware that just like your needs in life are always changing, so are your needs when it comes to online dating.

In fact, it may take you some time to actually figure out what it is you're looking for. You may spend what seem like countless hours perusing through databases of singles before you have an epiphany and obtain sudden clarity on what you really want in a mate. Then again, some people never have this epiphany and never really realize what draws them to one profile over another. The important thing is that you eventually wind up with someone special, but you may be able to speed up this process by periodically conducting a needs assessment.

Here are some great questions to ask yourself after you have been involved in online dating for a while:

- ♥ How has the process been going so far?

- ♥ What has definitely not worked for me?

- ♥ What has worked well?

- ♥ What have I learned about myself in this process so far?

- ♥ How can I make the process easier?

- ♥ Is this process working for me?

Be honest with yourself. This can be a great experience to not only meet someone special, but to also learn more about who you really are. Some people go their entire lives without ever conducting a self-evaluation. Much like filling out the initial dating profile questionnaire, the trick is to answer the questions as yourself and not as you *want* to be. If you have learned in the online dating process that you are only attracted to people who make at least as much money as you do, don't chalk this up to being shallow and dismiss it. Instead, acknowledge it as a personal truth and adjust your online dating practices accordingly. You want to find someone who is compatible with *you*, not compatible with the "Politically Correct You" that you want to portray.

Everything is a learning experience. You may have to hone your methods and do some real self-evaluation before you meet the person who is truly compatible with you. In the end, however, this self-evaluation is completely worth it if it brings you closer to finding your match.

If you have problems with this process, visit the self-help section of your local bookstore. There are plenty of books lined along the shelves that will help you with the process of self-actualization and realizing who you really are. After all, how can you know what you are really looking for if you don't know who you really are?

Changing Sites

You should never feel as though you have to stick with a particular dating site if you are dissatisfied with your current site. Even if you paid for a membership that still has a couple of months left before it expires, if you aren't satisfied with the layout of the site or the selection of singles within the database, it's time to dump the site and move on to greener pastures.

Before you post a profile on a different dating site, ask yourself two questions: What is it you liked about the previous site, and what was it that you didn't like? If you know what you liked, then you'll know to look for on another site, and if you know what you didn't like then you can steer clear of sites with similar features. For example, if you liked the compatibility tools with **www.Chemistry.com,** but didn't like how you couldn't gain access to the full database of singles, look to another dating Web site that features compatibility tools and also allows you the opportunity to sift through the database at your leisure.

The truth is that every dating Web site has something unique about it, whether it's the variety of singles or the general ambience of the site. One may offer features you like, but there may still be something you don't care for. If this is the case, then there is nothing wrong with trying out a different site. Keep in mind that other than any membership dues you agreed to, you certainly don't owe allegiance to any site in particular.

Periodically peruse sites you haven't tried out yet to see if they have something that the site (or sites) you already use does not have. Because you never really know what dating site the love of your life may be using, it is certainly worth it to have a look around. You may also want to go back and review sites you once tried but did not care for if you have been dating online for some time. It may be that when you initially started looking at online dating sites, some of the sites seemed more complicated than others. Now that you have more online dating experience under your belt, you may find that the features you considered complicated or confusing on these sites are actually quite easily navigated now that you know a little more about what you are doing.

A Little Help From Your Friends

Your friends and family can be a great resource to help you sift through singles databases as well as review the profiles of the people who initiate contact with you. If you aren't having much luck with finding the right people online, you may want to consider allowing a trusted friend or family member to join in the process. Invite your friend to look through the listing of compatible singles within the database and pick out some of the people who seem good for you.

Sometimes, friends and family can see things that we cannot. You may have a tendency to gravitate toward a certain type of volatile person, but you never really realized it. That's when someone who cares about you can step in and say, "Sure, that profile looks interesting, but have you considered this one right here?" The fact is that once in a while, a trusted friend or family member may actually be *better* at choosing a match for you than you are.

If your online search for a match has not yielded any suitable results after a period of time, consider allowing a friend to view all the suitable matches for you on the dating site you use and select a few for you to contact. This can be a fun way to find out who your friends think you are suitable for and also to consider some matches who you may not have looked twice at before. It's like getting set up on a blind date by someone who cares about you, only in a modern, technological way.

CASE STUDY: MEG'S STORY

"I was a 24-year-old female coming out of a long-term relationship, trying to navigate the dating scene in Philadelphia. I was dating people I met through friends or at social functions, like the city's music scene, and found them all falling a little short. I was out on a date with a friend of a friend and while our conversation was stilted and he didn't get my jokes, we finally bonded on something that no two people should ever bond over during a first date: previous relationships. As we lamented past wrongs, he mentioned that he had met his last girlfriend on a vegetarian dating site, **www.VeggieConnection.com**. He said this in passing, but I took note of the name of the site (another sure sign this relationship wasn't going places). Although I have been a vegetarian for more than ten years, I had never had a relationship with a vegetarian guy. I liked the thought of narrowing down the choices to some like-minded people. It was an easy site to use and do searches on, and best of all, it was free! New to the Internet dating game, I wasn't sure if I wanted to invest and VeggieConnection allows free profiles, with the option of paid subscriptions in order to send messages. As a free user, I could receive and answer messages from paid subscribers.

I was on VeggieConnection for a few weeks, mostly receiving messages from the 40+ crowd, a couple of Swedish guys, and many men from India. I began talking to some people around my age, having brief e-mail conversations through the site. But then one person's introductory e-mail really got my attention. It said, 'Saw your profile and it looks like you may have a thing or two to say about the world.' Rather than referring to my looks or trying to sell himself with a dating sales-pitch, he actually seemed interested in what I had to say.

And boy, did we have a lot to say to each other. Kevin and I bonded over discussions about education (we're both teachers), life philosophies, and humorous tangents. We talked for a month and a half, graduating from e-mail to hours of phone conversations before deciding to meet in person — which presented a bit of a problem. Kevin is from Connecticut, and I am from Pennsylvania, which means we live about three hours apart. We decided on a halfway point, a town in New Jersey with a Victorian, castle-like mansion in a park to meet for the first time.

CASE STUDY: MEG'S STORY

As I drove, I called my date to see how his trip was going — he was already there! He was an hour early, which didn't make me any less nervous, knowing he was sitting there waiting. I arrived, stepped out of the car, and there he was, no longer just a voice or a photograph. We hit it off well, conversing comfortably, touring the mansion, and walking around the park until it was time for lunch.

We drove through the small New Jersey town looking for a place two vegetarians on a first date could find some lunch. We passed by a steakhouse and some fast-food joints, then hit the downtown area. Not having seen any vegetarian-friendly places, we parked and decided to walk around, figuring we'd run into some sort of restaurant. As we rounded the corner out of the parking lot, a sign grabbed our attention: 'Veggie Heaven.' A vegetarian restaurant! That's when we knew it was meant to be.

The date stretched into a full day, 10 hours of conversation. Seven months later, we are still going strong, visiting each other every weekend and on holidays. I never expected to find love on the Internet, but I don't think I could have found someone who I am more compatible with. Sometimes the person you're supposed to be with just doesn't happen to live next door, or even in the same state."

CHAPTER 11

Your Happy Ending

How do you know when you have actually met the person of your dreams? Refer to your past relationships before you decide that you are head-over-heels for someone you meet online. In other words, if you have a propensity toward falling in love quickly (and then quickly falling back out of love), then you may not want to assume that the quick emotions you develop for someone you meet online are authentic. Take the time to make sure the feelings are valid. Conversely, if you are the type of person who rarely falls in love, but you start to feel feelings of love toward someone you meet online, this is certainly something that should make you sit up and take notice.

A lot depends on the geographic proximity of the special someone you meet online. If you hook up with someone who lives fairly close to you, allowing you to meet up a few times a week, feelings of love can be authentic. If the person you hook up with online happens to live a thousand miles away and the two of you are limited to phone calls and e-mails, feelings of love that you develop can indeed be authentic, but it is best to meet the person face-to-face before you make the decision that you are actually in love.

This is certainly not to say that people who meet face-to-face will always cultivate a loving relationship, nor does it suggest that two people who have a long-distance relationship are doomed to not genuinely fall in love until they can physically be together. Instead, it merely points out the fact that sometimes, being around someone is a lot different than talking to someone over the phone or via e-mail. There are things that can become obvious (good or bad) when you physically spend time with someone.

Long-Distance Relationships

Long-distance relationships can work, but they can also take a lot of extra effort. There are benefits to long-distance relationships, especially for people who prefer some time alone or who start to quickly feel smothered when spending too much time with another person. Additionally, some people may reveal intimate details of their lives more openly and quickly when the majority of conversations take place over the phone or through messages online. It can simply be easier to talk about sensitive subjects — like details of a divorce or past medical issues — when these subjects aren't discussed face-to-face. This is not true for all people, as there are some people who would never entertain the idea of broaching sensitive topics unless they were physically with someone, but for some, distance can soften the blow of topics that are difficult or painful to discuss.

If you find yourself involved in a long-distance relationship as a result of online dating, take solace in the fact that many people have been through the same thing before many of them had their happy endings. It is not unheard of for a couple dating online for a while to eventually wind up living together or married as long as one or both of the people are willing to relocate. You *can* wind up happily involved with someone who does not live nearby. It is up to you whether this situation appeals to you or not, but there is nothing wrong with giving it a try to see how things develop.

How do you know that your long-distance relationship is a success? If you have no desire to date anyone else, and you know the other person feels the same way too, this can be a good sign that the relationship is heading in a good direction. Should you cancel your online dating membership and pack your bags to go move closer to the other person? Don't jump into anything without thinking it through, and don't entertain the idea of quitting your job, selling your house, and saying goodbye to all your friends in order to move a thousand miles away to be closer to someone who you may not even really know. If you and the other person decide that you're both in love with each other and you're ready to take the relationship a step further, do so with the knowledge that there will be some adjusting necessary for both of you to switch from a relationship where you hardly ever see each other to suddenly seeing each other every day.

"I Love You!"

After spending a great deal of time getting to know the person you met online, you both decide that you're going to date each other exclusively and that you are both in love with each other. Congratulations! The question now becomes whether the two of you should cancel your online dating memberships or instead allow them to simply lapse while you both continue with your blissful relationship.

There are arguments both ways. While some may say that canceling your online dating membership is a sign of commitment and devotion, others may say that you should just keep the membership active if you have already prepaid a certain number of months. After all, if you paid for a six-month membership, and have already fallen in love in month four, what is the harm in leaving the membership active for the final two months?

The problem is that sometimes people fall into a pattern with online dating. Although they may meet someone special and fall in love, there is always the idea in the back of their minds that maybe there is someone better waiting for them online.

They may miss the fun of sifting through profiles and looking to see who is out there. This does not happen to everyone, but if it happens to you, then you need to take a hard look at the situation and decide the best course of action for you to take.

If you are the type of person who jumps into something feet-first and gets thoroughly involved in what you're doing, you may have developed a real love for online dating. You might relish the process of looking through the database of singles and maybe even enjoyed the "thrill of the hunt" that comes with selecting people to correspond with. If this sounds like you, you might find that it's a little harder than you thought it would be to no longer be involved with online dating. When the membership is still valid, even if you aren't using it, you know it's there and that you have the option to hop online and get right back into the swing of things if you would like.

Don't be surprised if — even though you have found someone you really care for — you find yourself occasionally logging on to look around and see who has added profiles into the database. It may not even be that you're looking to meet some-one beyond the person you have already met, and you may be perfectly happy with your relationship, but old habits can die hard. If this is the situation you're in, you need to recognize two important things: First of all, the person you're in the re-lationship with may not be happy to discover that you still oc-casionally log on and have a look around the same dating site you used to meet each other. This can be the type of thing that can end a relationship, or at the very least, can certainly damage the trust within the relationship. Secondly, ending your membership with the online dating site may be the last step you take before fully committing to the relationship. If you indeed decide to shut off your membership, this is a big move that should be celebrated if it's in conjunction with meeting someone special.

Don't cancel your membership with a dating site that you like if you have just a couple of successful dates with someone you meet online. You may have an inkling that this person may be your match, but until you're more sure of your feelings, there is nothing wrong with maintaining the membership (especially if it is already paid for). You don't have to log in to the site and peruse the database of singles, and you don't even have to check your messages and reply to people attempting to initiate contact. Just don't rush to cancel a membership subscription that you may wind up using again in the near future.

Remember that some of the online dating Web sites allow other users to see how long it has been since you logged in to your account, so if you try to sneak a peek at your messages while involved in a new relationship, your partner may be able to see this — and it probably will not be a good thing.

CASE STUDY: SETH AND TRUDY'S STORY

This success story appears courtesy of **www.JDate.com.**

Dear JDate,

I had been on and off JDate a couple of times — a month here, a month there — scanning the world for possibilities because it didn't seem as though "she" was living in South Florida near me. I felt I had the right approach — you needed a good sense of humor if you were going to put your faith and future on the line for each date with someone you only knew through the Web.

Reading the profiles was often humorous — nothing personal, just that everyone I read about was "laidback, worked out, and could enjoy an evening dressed up or in jeans." I was looking for a woman who was a little more creative, had a little more of an edge, and enjoyed taking risks.

Was I in for a surprise! I realized that just dating only online might not work for me. It might be great for others, but I needed to see a woman's smile and feel that vibe when you just know. So, my brother and I took off for a JDate Travel adventure at Club Med® Cancun. What could be better than a little sun, a little drinking, a little dancing, and hanging with a group of Jews? It was actually the second trip we went on. My brother plays guitar for Club Med when he's not taking care of kids at Children's National Hospital in D.C. (and yes, ladies, he is available, but is still a little JDate-shy), so it was easy for us to mingle and make friends. The pressure was off. Everyone was having a great time relaxing. It almost seemed as though meeting "the one" was not the priority. And we all know what happens when you're not looking...

Our story really didn't start off all that romantically. We were three days into our five-day July 4th trip when fate took over. My brother had an unfortunate accident — he fell off the stage while finishing his first set at an outdoor dinner by the ocean. It was a long night in a Mexican hospital trying to speak Spanish, and my brother had an emergency ankle surgery plus plenty of painkillers. I was wheeling him past the Club Med front desk the next afternoon, ready to get back to the party and shake off the night, when Trudy walked up. I hadn't seen her yet on the trip. Trudy had heard what had happened. She stopped us before heading in to town to make sure my brother was OK. We found out later that she stopped us just to get a closer look at me.

Later that night, after enjoying some great guitar, Trudy and I finally got a chance to talk, and we haven't stopped since. We spent hours that night getting to know one another and then all the next day — 36 fantastic hours together before it

CASE STUDY: SETH AND TRUDY'S STORY

was time to leave. I headed back to South Florida, and she headed back home to Los Angeles. She slipped a note in my back pocket and told me not to read it until I got on the plane. The anticipation was killing me, but I waited. Of course, I still have that first note.

Before she landed in L.A., we had made plans to see each other again. Most would assume that our distance alone would make being together impossible, but I had found my beautiful Jewish princess who was creative, had that extra little edge, and, fortunately, took risks.

Four months later, after long weekends in L.A., visits to South Florida, visits to her hometown of Vancouver, and trips to D.C. to hang out with my brother (whom we owe this all to), Trudy packed up her wonderful L.A. life and took one last risk. She risked everything she had for us and moved in with me. We got engaged after nine months and were married in March 2007. She is my soul mate.

My life has never been so fulfilled, so complete, so risk-free. There is so much more to tell, and this is only the beginning.

Trudy and I have been happily married for more than a year and a half now, hosting a beautiful wedding with friends and family in Whistler for skiing and Vancouver's Stanley Park for the ceremony/wedding. We currently live in Hollywood, Florida, and are expecting our first child in about two weeks. We can't wait to welcome our little girl into our home. We are working toward becoming a bi-coastal family so we can live closer to Trudy's family for part of the year. She is still pushing me to think outside the box and enjoy life as much as possible, and I love her for it. You only live once. You only love like this once. Go for it!

Thank you!

Seth and Trudy
Hollywood, Florida and Los Angeles, California

CONCLUSION

J ust like the traditional dating scene, online dating can have its share of ups and downs. Whatever approach you take with online dating — whether it is a highly analytical approach or a wait-and-see approach — there is an excellent chance that when all is said and done, you will have some great stories to tell. The hope is that you will also meet the person of your dreams.

Your match is out there. Getting involved in online dating is a great method to use when you want to increase the odds of meeting someone special. It is an exciting process and also a process that has yielded successful results for many people.

Go into Internet dating with an open mind and an optimistic viewpoint. Keep in mind this great quote from French novelist Henri B. Stendhal: *A very small degree of hope is sufficient to cause the birth of love.* Are you ready for your "birth of love?"

APPENDIX

http://dating.personals.yahoo.com – Yahoo! Personals – Free search

www.match.com – Free to look; offers a personality test through **www.Chemistry.com**

www.FriendFinder.com – Only free to join; offers a search

www.date.com- Free to join; offers a search; uses live web video and instant messaging

www.MustLovePets.com – For animal lovers; can be a basic member, but if you pay you can send messages to other singles

www.Lovetropolis.com – $17.95 fee for a lifetime

www.MillionaireMatch.com – For financially successful individuals; membership rates as follows:

- 12 months for $179.95
- Six months for $119.95
- Three months for $74.95
- One month for $39.95

Marriage-Minded Sites

www.perfectmatch.com – Can review matches for free; free compatibility test

SUBSCRIPTION PLAN	
One-Month Subscription	$59.95
Two-Month Subscription	$79.90
Three-Month Subscription	$110.85
Six-Month Subscription	$173.70

SUBSCRIPTION PLAN	RENEWAL RATE
One-Month Subscription	Same as the initial payment
Two-Month Subscription	$29.95 per month
Three-Month Subscription	$29.95 per month
Four-Month Subscription	$29.95 per month
Six-Month Subscription	$24.95 per month

www.eHarmony.com – Compatibility matching

www.Matchmaker.com – Free matchmaking profile

www.Chemistry.com –Personality test; provides matches

Religious Services

http://ChristianCafe.com – Provides search; free trial

MEMBERSHIP RATES (All prices are in US dollars)		
Two Weeks	$29.95	Only $2.14/day
One Month	$34.95	Only $1.17/day
Three Months	$49.95	Only 56 cents/day
Six Months	$79.95	Only 44 cents/day
One Year	$109.95	Only 30 cents/day

www.BigChurch.com – A local search; basic membership is free, then price goes up

www.JDate.com – Free membership; for low fee you can gain more privileges

www.JewishFriendFinder.com – Free basic membership; provides search

www.Fusion101.com – Free; for Christians; provides a local search

www.LDSPlanet.com – Latter-Day Saints can meet here; payment is required to see contacts

www.ChristianCupid.com

www.Muslima.com

Ethnic

www.BlackMatch.com – Still under construction

http://Amigos.com – Provides a search; basic membership is free

www.BlackSingles.com – Helps match with a personality profile; fee to join and look at matches

www.LatinAmericanCupid.com

www.AfroIntroductions.com

www.AsianEuro.com

www.AussieCupid.com.au

www.BBWCupid.com

www.BlackCupid.com

www.BrazilCupid.com

www.CaribbeanCupid.com

www.ChineseLoveLinks.com

www.ColombianCupid.com

www.DominicanCupid.com

www.FilipinaHeart.com

www.HongKongCupid.com

www.IndianCupid.com

www.IndonesianCupid.com

www.InterracialCupid.com

www.IranianSinglesConnection.com

www.JapanCupid.com

www.KoreanCupid.com

www.LatinAmericanCupid.com

www.MexicanCupid.com

www.RussianEuro.com

www.SingaporeLoveLinks.com

www.SouthAfricanCupid.com

www.ThaiLoveLinks.com

www.UkraineDate.com

www.VietnamCupid.com

Senior Dating

www.SeniorMatch.com – Four membership purchase options:

- 12 months for $143.95
- Six months for $95.95
- Three months for $59.95
- One month for $29.95

http://SeniorFriendFinder.com

Gay

http://ProudSingles.net – Compatibility matching system; free to e-mail other users

http://OutPersonals.com – For gay men; join for Free

http://GayFriendFinder.com – For gay men; join for free

www.gay.com – Join for free or for premium

www.GayCupid.com – Join for free; search

www.PinkCupid.com – For lesbian dating

Free:

www.Lavalife.com - Provides video chat, search

www.Fringles.com

www.Plentyoffish.com – Provides chemistry test

www.OKCupid.com

www.Mingles.com – Just a search, not compatibility

www.PassionsNetwork.com – Just a search, but considered a niche dating site

www.ECPersonals.com – International personal ads directory

www.PricelessPartner.com – For love or friendship

www.FervorSingles.com – Search based on zip code

www.SayMeHi.com – Search based on zip code

www.DateHookup.com

BIBLIOGRAPHY

Berry, Diane M. *Romancing the Web: A Therapist's Guide to the Finer Points of Online Dating.* Blue Water Publications, 2005.

Dailey, Shane. *Slow and Tight: Every Man's Guide to Online Dating ... Simplified!* BookSurge Publishing, 2008.

<http://www.chemistry.com>

<http://www.eharmony.com>

<http://www.jdate.com>

<http://www.latimes.com/features/lifestyle/la-ig-dating 28-2008dec28,0,1563805.story?page=2>

<http://www.match.com>

<http://www.perfectmatch.com>

<http://www.reuters.com/article/lifestyleMolt/
idUSTRE4B73X520081208>

<http://www.time.com/time/business/
article/0,8599,1868694,00.html>

Koppel, Dale. *The Intelligent Woman's Guide to Online Dating.*
Peterman Samuelson, 2008.

Silverstein, MD, Judith and Michael Lasky, JD. *Online Dating
for Dummies. A Reference for the Rest of Us.* Wiley, Indianapolis,
2004.

AUTHOR BIOGRAPHY

Tamsen Butler is an experienced writer and editor. In addition to using her degree in psychology to analyze relationships, online and otherwise, she also writes about personal finance topics for a variety of online publications. She was also a contributing author to the book *Get Satisfied: How Twenty People Like You Found the Satisfaction of Enough*.

INDEX

D

E

F

G

H

I

T

U

W

Y

More Great Titles

shing

How to Use the Internet to Get Your Next Job

In this book, learn how to conduct an effective job search by determining keywords, creating and format and mastering on Perhaps most import job search sites we h are the major sites, Jobs, and CareerBui sites for every ind harness the powerful the Internet to find yo what industry or level.

ISBN 13: 978-1-60138-239-9 • $21.95

How to Use Social Networking on the Web to Market & Promote Your Business or Service — *With Little or No Money*

Learn how to use Internet social networks as a marketing tool, allowing your businesses to reach out and touch target demographics like never before. Details about Facebook and MySpace as the two biggest sources of potential new customers, along with why this is not a fad but a fundamental shift in how business should be done.

978-1-60138-317-4 • $24.95

The MySpace.com Handbook:
The Complete Guide for Members and Parents

MySpace.com is a free, social networking site that allows members to share photos, and participate in tips to creating MySpace profile overview of step instructions safety issues, and also a chapter who may want to products.

ISBN 13: 978-1-60138-121-7 • $24.95

The Online Identity Theft Prevention Kit: *Stop Scammers, Hackers, and Identity Thieves from Ruining Your Life*

Reduce online identity theft with this up-to-the-minute book. You will find valuable expertise to evaluate and determine your, your family's, and your business's risks. The books has a detailed plan so that you can take action for prevention now. There is also a step-by-step program detailing what to do if your identity has been stolen, plus numerous letters, templates and forms.

ISBN 13: 978-1-60138-008-1 • $24.95

To order call toll-free **800-814-1132** or visit **www.atlantic-pub.com**